Ordinary Life, Extraordinary God

THE LIFE STORY OF DAVID MAX LEE

ISBN: 1470168766
ISBN 13: 9781470168766

Introduction

My first thought in writing the story of my life is to praise the Lord for his grace and mercy in calling me to himself. The next thought is hope that this will encourage our grandchildren or anyone else who may read this story.

My story is not one of high adventure and great spiritual victories. I am just a person who believes in the Lord Jesus Christ—ordinary life, extraordinary God. I love how God's word expresses what he has done and continues to do in my life: 2 Corinthians 5:17, "Therefore, if anyone is in Christ he is a new creation; the old has gone, the new has come!" Colossians 1:13-14, " For he has rescued us from the dominion of darkness and brought us into the kingdom of the Son he loves, in whom we have redemption the forgiveness of sins."

Cover photos: Background is Valley Haven Farm, about 1940; Front: David with horses, Bonnie and Lady; Dave and Margaret in front of Victory Bible Camp dining hall, 1954. Back: Johnny Gillespie baptizing Dave in Shallow Lake at Victory Bible Camp, 1953.

Acknowledgements

I want to thank everyone who helped with this project. It has been a long process, with many people involved. In no particular order, I wish to thank Jewell Joslen for her encouragement to write my story and for typing many pages of handwritten notes. My daughter, Sharon Beachy, and grandchildren, Melissa Schroeder and Rachel Beachy, put in hours of editing, formatting and thought. Thanks also to my sons, Brian and Dan Lee, for their input, especially when my memory wasn't always accurate. My sincere thanks to all. To the rest of my family, thank-you for your love and support. I hope that I remembered everyone, and if not, I apologize for the oversight.

Childhood On The Farm

I like to say that I was crowded to Christ because it was all God's doing. I wasn't searching for God. What an amazing God, who chooses and reaches out to us. The story of how God drew me to himself began years earlier.

I was born March 17, 1922, in my grandparents' farm home to Charles and Orpah Lee. I feel it was a great privilege to be born into this family and raised in the beautiful, rolling hills of southern Indiana.

When I was two, we moved to the farm where I grew up, Valley Haven Farm, near Bedford, Indiana. This was a wonderful place for me to live. My grandparents on my father's side, Alfred and Phoebe Lee, lived on the adjoining farm south of us and my mother's parents, Thomas and Mary Fields, lived on the adjoining farm to the north. I could walk to either farm. There were cousins at each home and I always felt welcomed, especially at Grandpa Lee's farm. He really liked us kids. Grandpa Fields was much older—he was born in 1850 and died in 1933.

My earliest memory is the day my sister was born—November 24, 1925. Donna Charlene was born at home in the house where we grew up. I was told that I would have a brother or sister that day and was taken to Pop's house to await the new arrival. (Pop was my grandfather Lee.) When I arrived home to see my little sister I was very disappointed to find that she could not come out to play with me. Play time would come later.

Donna and I agree that we were privileged to have parents who loved us and were honest and hard-working, took us to church and Sunday school, were involved in community activities and set an example of working together. Their lives left a lasting impression on us to this day.

My father, Charles Alexander Lee was born August 2, 1891 and died at age 79 on September 3, 1970. My mother, Rose Orpah Lillian Fields Lee lived to be 91, from October 27, 1895 to January 26, 1987. She was the eighth in a family ten children. My parents were married December, 24, 1914. Dad was twenty-two and Mother nineteen.

Our parents gave us a secure home and we never doubted their love for us. They set a good example of honesty, integrity and hard work. My parents were outgoing, friendly people and had many friends among our neighbors. Dad was a hardworking farmer his whole life and that is all he ever did. The farm was his *occupation*, his *recreation*, and his *hobby* all in one setting. He really enjoyed what he was doing, in spite of hardship and trials through the years.

Growing up on the farm in the 20's and 30's was a unique time. Life was very simple, but times were changing as housing improved, and farming advanced from mules and horses to tractors and mechanized harvesting. We lived in an older house with no running water, no electricity and no indoor bathroom. There was no insulation in our home either. We heated with a wood-burning heater and a wood-burning cook stove. Light was from kerosene or Aladdin lamps—poor sources of light.

How do I express in words the sights, the sounds and the smells of the farm during my growing up years? The farm was a lovely sight with all the fields and woodlands, the cattle, sheep, chickens, geese, turkeys, and other critters. Each animal and bird had its own distinct sound and smell. There was also the lovely scent of fruit tree blossoms, especially on Pop's farm with many acres of apples, pears, peaches and cherries. The fruit trees attracted a large number of nesting birds which added their songs to the sound of the farm.

The farm was situated in a lovely area of rolling hills, near the little settlement of Leesville. Crops were planted along the base of the hills on the flatter "bottom" land near Guthrie Creek. The forested hills were a valuable asset to the farm, as a place for recreation and hunting, a source of firewood and a timber sale from time to time. Guthrie Creek gave us much pleasure for fishing, swimming and ice skating in winter.

After work on summer days we swam in an area that we called the swimming hole, down behind the barn.

Each season had its uniqueness, but I enjoyed it all. It was a lovely place in spring with the flowers blooming, especially on Grandpa Lee's farm. Summer was often hot and humid, but much was happening, with planting, watching the seeds come to life, and then cultivating to keep the weeds under control. Late summer, with the help of neighbors, was the time for wheat harvest. Then in the fall we harvested the corn and filled the silo. Winter was a time for working in the woods, cutting firewood and logging.

Living on the farm was a year around occupation and our lives were filled with much hard work, often with shovels and pitchforks. I can't remember a time when I was not working in the field with my father. I was just a freckled-faced skinny kid and not too strong. I can remember being so tired each morning I could hardly get moving.

Dad used two kinds of plows to work the fields—a walking plow and a riding plow. I was way too small to use them, so dad fixed a shorter step on the riding plow for my feet so I could follow him in the field. A problem I had was if I turned too sharp at the corners it would tip over.

We each had a team of mules for plowing. We would walk in a furrow holding onto the plow handles to guide it as it sliced through dirt. Dad had a team of huge mules. They were very smart, as they had discovered that if they walked close together it would cause the plow to cut half of what it was supposed to plow and this made it pull easier. Dad would see this and come over to straighten them out. When dad took the lines their ears stood straight up and they marched right along. The mules got toughened to the work and before it got too hot we would go at a steady pace all day long. With the two teams and plows we could plow four acres a day. That doesn't sound like much compared to today's farming method. We just kept on working until we got the job done.

Dad usually kept five or six work animals. If we needed more horse power we could borrow some from Pop. One time dad borrowed a horse, old Maud, to work with Kate, the mule. As I was hitching up to the harrow, Maud was off on one side so the trace chain would not reach the single tree. I gave Maud a gentle tap with the trace chain to make her step over it. When I did this she kicked and hit me right in the stomach with her huge hoof. This knocked the breath out of me and sent me flying into the plowed ground. When dad saw me lying in the dirt he thought Kate had done it, so he started whipping her before I could get my breath back. I soon recovered and went to work. That old nag Maud worked just fine after that.

✖ A friend once mentioned that everything we did had a handle on it: shovels, pitchforks, hoes, plow handles and other items we used at that time. I remember so well how my hands would swell on Sunday when we were not working. It would take some time on Monday morning to get the swelling down. I really did enjoy working on the farm in spite of the hard work involved. It was a good feeling as I grew older and stronger, to be able to do the work of a grown man.

As an example of the life we lived, one Saturday we went to Bedford for supplies and came home in mid-afternoon. I thought we would have some free time, but no, Dad said, "Let's get to work". So we rounded up and harnessed the mules and drove to the farthest part of the farm where we had been working previously. We worked two hours, then returned home, unharnessed the mules and did the evening chores. He just could not rest knowing there was work to be done. That is another good memory of my father. One thing about my dad was he was always out there working harder than the rest of us. While the work was hard and hot at times, I never felt abused. I was only doing what most farm kids did in those days.

One of the jobs I dreaded most was putting up the hay. Almost all hay was put up loose at that time. This required lots of work with the pitch fork. Later we bought a hay loader which gathered the hay from windrows on the ground and elevated it up onto the wagon. This was an improvement over the pitch fork method. At the barn the hay was off-loaded by means of a grapple fork. The fork lifted the hay from the wagon and was operated by a long rope and pulley mechanism system. There was a long track at the peak of the roof. The fork load of hay was pulled up by a team at the other end of the barn. When the first load of hay reached the top it locked into the carrier which ran the length of the barn and the hay could be dumped by the man on the wagon with a trip rope. It was a hot job especially for the man in the loft up next to the roof.

There were times of toil and struggle, especially the depression years of the 1930's and the drought years of 1934-36. We were very poor during those years, but so were all of our neighbors. Our diet was very simple but we never went hungry. We ate what we raised in a large garden and had meat from hogs, chickens and beef. My mother would can hundreds of quarts of fruit, beans, pickles and meat.

Though I didn't know it at the time, I had some experiences of God's protection. One day I was with my Dad when he was spreading manure. Somehow I fell off the manure spreader seat and got caught between a single tree and double tree right behind the mules hitched to the spreader. Now this mule team was prone to buck and kick at anything. Dad got me out of danger and the mules stayed calm. The Lord gave his protection when I could have been killed. This team was soon sold and replaced with more dependable mules.

Another time I got pneumonia and was very sick, even unconscious for a time. This happened after I went ice skating with a cousin on a neighbor's pond. While skating I got hot, then on the way home I became chilled, which led to becoming ill. Our doctor came to the house to give treatment. I remember when I began to feel better, that one day dad came in to see how I was feeling and put his big calloused hand on my forehead to offer his comfort. Again, my life was spared.

Then there was a grapevine accident, when I was in the field working with Dad. Donna and I discovered a wild grapevine that had grown up a large tree. By cutting the vine at the ground we could use it like a rope and swing out over a steep hill. That time when I pulled the vine loose from the tree it came right off. I fell down the hill and landed on some rocks and got a cut under my chin. No bones were broken, but some of my teeth were cracked. When the bleeding stopped Dad put me on a mule and we rode to the house.

I did not feel too good for a few days, with my neck and face swollen, and eating was painful. This was the last time Donna went to the field with us. While this accident may not have been life threatening, it could have been much worse, considering the distance that I fell. I still can feel a small scar under my chin.

Even though our lifestyle was very simple and there was much work to do, our parents cared for us and provided things for our enjoyment. When we were young they gave us a dog named Stubby that was half Saint Bernard and half collie. He was a huge dog that followed us everywhere. He was also a good stock dog that could bring in the cows when told to do so—sometimes on the run. Dad made a harness for the dog so he could pull us around in a small wagon. One time Donna and I were in the front pasture with Stubby pulling us in the wagon, when mother called the dog. Stubby took off in high gear and jumped the front yard fence. The dog landed on one side and the wagon stayed on the other! We were dumped out, but no harm was done.

They also got a goat for us to play with. Dad built a harness for this animal as well, so she could pull a two-wheeled cart that we rode around in. One time mother sent Donna and me up the road to meet a peddler that came around with a truck filled with items to sell. She loaded a case of eggs into the goat cart for us to use in buying supplies. All went well until the goat saw the peddler's "store on wheels". We had a difficult time controlling the goat and keeping the case of eggs from toppling over. We did manage it, but the peddler thought it was the funniest thing he had seen in a long time. On our return home we had to descend a steep hill and had no brakes. We improvised by putting a broom handle through the spokes, to lock the wheels. It was an exciting ride, but we made it safely home.

Typical farm-boy look: freckled and wearing overalls.

Charles and Orpah Lee.

Charles riding the mule, Belle.

School Days (1928-1939)

School time was a real turning point in my life. The school I attended was named Root School after Harvey Root on whose farm the school was built. It was one mile from our house to the school. To get there I had to walk, as there were no school buses for us. From our house I would go past our barn, across Guthrie Creek, past the Root's barn and house and then on to school.

Sometimes my dad would carry me across the creek if the water was too deep for me to wade. Other times I would go down the county road and cross the creek on the bridge. From there I would walk across the bottom land and on past Mr. Root's place to the school. This almost doubled the distance. I walked with the four daughters from the Walker Brown family. I can't think of any particular danger on the way even though we walked in all kinds of weather. Sometimes when it was cold the creek would freeze over and we could cross on the ice.

The school was a little white one-room building. My first grade teacher was Trilla Glover from Leesville, who taught all eight grades. Miss Glover was very kind to me. After three years at the Root School the county provided a school bus and transported us to the school in the little town of Fort Ritner. The Root school was closed and is now a private home. The school at Fort Ritner was a brick two room school with two teachers: Miss Moon taught the first four grades and Glenn Weaver the next four grades.

It seems that from day one I found school a very difficult thing to handle. I was a scared, timid kid, and very fearful if called upon to go up front to do some work on the blackboard. I think I have blocked out some memories of going to school since it was such a trial for me. My mother told me in later years that she had to give me a whipping each morning for two weeks to make me go to school. As I try to write about my school days I find it difficult to put in words this experience which impacted my life for many years to come. I always felt uncomfortable around crowds of people and felt like I was being watched, for whatever reason I do not know.

Having said all of this I did learn to cope somewhat with the fact I had to go to school, though I was not a happy kid there. I have pondered over the years as to what caused my feelings about school and being around people. Was it my fault? Was it an inherited trait? Or was it caused by some experience in my life? I can never come up with any real reason for all of my distress. I was not picked on or abused at school.

I did learn to read and made passing grades even though I didn't work very hard at it. I was not stupid and managed to pass on to the next grade. All through the eight grades of school I continued to have problems of insecurity. I can remember one teacher at the Fort Ritner School speaking to me as I was standing by watching the other kids play. He asked me why I didn't go play with the other kids. He said it in a nice way to encourage me to be more active.

Most days I asked myself, "When will this day end so I can be at home?" I felt secure and comfortable at home. My parents were kind to me. Donna and I always got along very well.

After the eighth grade I went on to high school at Tunnelton. My problems in school continued and even got worse all through high school. By the time I got to my senior year each day was pure misery. I was failing in one of my classes for the first time and I didn't care. At this point in time I was thinking that I could not continue in school. I was literally in bondage to fear. Many times after a day in school I would be so sick to my stomach that when I got off the bus at home I would throw up. Then I was fine. I thank God for deliverance from the bondage of fear.

After Christmas break I told my parents that I did not want to go back to school. This really disappointed my mother and father, especially my mother. They talked earnestly with me to go back, but I stayed home. At this point in my life no matter what decision I made there were real problems, though staying at home looked better. So at seventeen, in 1939, I was a high school drop-out, which I am not proud of.

In contrast, my parents were outgoing people and had many friends. I remember my mother and her brother, my Uncle Ralph, would sing occasionally at funerals. Dad was involved in community affairs for many years. My sister Donna went to school to have a good time and she did, much to the distress of my mother. I can remember my mother sitting down with Donna to help her catch up with homework when she was getting behind in school.

My parents were active in church and community events and an outgoing couple who had many friends. There were many times during the 1930's that a group of young people would come to our home for games and fun like pulling taffy. This was during the Great Depression years when there was little money to be had. It didn't cost much to come to our house for a good time. Some walked, some came on bicycles, one fellow had an old model-T car, while my cousin, Paul, had a small car. They would gather up some of the young ladies in the community and come to the party. My parents made the young people welcome and Dad was actually the life of the party. He was a fun-loving guy.

When World War II came along in 1941 this ended the young people coming to our home. It seemed everybody was involved in this great conflict. Some went into the armed services, others worked in factories; all were doing something to help in the war effort.

About this time, my mother joined a group of farm wives to sing as a chorus. I remember how much she enjoyed singing with this group and the fellowship they had. They would sing at different events. One time the chorus went to Toronto, Canada to sing. My father went along with my mother. He did not sing with the chorus, but put on Mother's choir robe and did some kind of act (not sure what it was), much to the amusement of the ladies and the embarrassment of my mother. They also sang for President Eisenhower during a stop in Indianapolis.

I am very thankful for my parents and the life they lived. They were just common people with very little formal education, but wise in how to live. For most of us when we leave this world we are soon forgotten, but God cares for His own. I am confident my parents' names are written down in the Lamb's Book of Life. They left a wonderful legacy for us and for that I am thankful.

Making Maple Syrup

In the late thirties my cousin Robert (Bob) lived on Grandfather Lee's farm. One winter we got the idea to make maple syrup. The trees were there to tap, but we needed equipment. Our neighbor, Everett McKeaigg, heard about what we wanted to do so he offered to give us some old fashioned wooden sap buckets that his family had used many years before. Another neighbor, Auk Brown, had a nice pan we could use. For spouts to tap into the trees we used homemade ones which were hollowed out alder shrubs.

During the last of January, Bob and I set up our operation in the woods, near the sugar maples. Bob had a team of horses we used to haul the sap into our little shed we had built over the pan. It was fun and we enjoyed the work. Aunt Anita, Bob's mother, helped. Several times she made pancakes which we ate as we watched the fire under the pan.

The next year I ordered some regular sap buckets, a filter and a thermometer. The new equipment really helped. We also had a larger pan made. In later years I continued to make maple syrup after Aunt Anita and cousin Bob moved on. My Uncle Ross and Aunt Gertie Lee retired to Grandfather Lee's farm. Uncle Ross was a good sales person so I made the syrup and Uncle Ross sold the product. I usually made 50-100 gallons each year.

One day I had a pan full of sap cooking when I heard a neighbor cutting timber a short distance away on his farm, so I thought I would go visit him while the sap continued to boil down. When I returned to the sugar house (what we called the building where we cooked) I heard the horses snorting and acting strange. When I got closer I could see smoke coming from the building instead of steam. I hurried into the shed and saw that all the sap had boiled away and left a baked-on mess in the pan. It took me several hours of hard cleaning to restore the pan. The heat had also melted the solder from the seams of the pan. Uncle Ralph was able to re-solder the seams so I could get back to work. Because of this accident we lost at least 5 gallons of syrup.

To haul the sap to the sugar house I used two horses pulling a sled with a tank. One day I decided that only one horse could easily pull the sled so I took Lady to do the work. Things worked well at first, but then Lady decided she wanted to go back to the barn with the other work animals. All of a sudden she took off in high gear. Soon the tank fell off spilling most of the sap. Then the single tree broke when the sled hung up on some trees. Lady kept on going until she got to the barn lot where I found her quietly waiting to be let through the gate.

Farm And Railroad Work

In the fall of 1939 a friend called us for help on harvesting his corn crop. Bruce Childers had taken a job in Indianapolis so was not in a position to complete his harvest. This we agreed to do as we had already finished our harvest. It was over three miles to the corn field to be harvested.

Dad and I each had a team and wagon for this job. We harnessed up before daylight to drive to the field just as it got light enough to see. This was all hard work, using what we called a shucking peg to shuck each ear of corn one at a time. We would shuck a full wagon load each morning and another load in the afternoon. We unloaded the wagon with a scoop shovel.

My Dad set a fast pace and I had to really work hard to keep up with him. We repeated this daily routine until the job was finished. I recall how cold my fingers would get on a frosty November morning, until the sun came up and melted the frost on the ears of corn.

In the spring of 1941 I got a job with the Western Union Telegraph Company through my Uncle Ross Lee. Uncle Ross and Aunt Gertie were cooks for the gang that I went to work with. This work was mainly with the New York Central Railroad providing telegraph service for the railroad. The crews stayed in rail cars. There were sleeping cars, a dining car, kitchen car, tool car, equipment car and a water car. Sometimes we had a pole train where there were five or six flatcars loaded with the telegraph poles that we rolled off at the location for a new pole to be installed.

This was my first work away from home and a new experience. Sometimes we worked away from our railcar headquarters so we ate in a restaurant. I had never eaten in a restaurant before and had no idea what to order. The menu might as well have been written in Greek for all it meant to me. One fellow worker ordered a hamburger steak so I did the same. That went down real good so I ordered hamburger steak several times until I learned how to order.

Norman Stewart, Joe Parkman, Clyde Speer, Jim Fish, my cousins Lee Jean and Lyle Roberts, Bill Starr and myself were all recruits Uncle Ross rounded up from our area. They called us the Back Creek gang. My job was to dig holes and help set the telegraph poles. To me this was easy compared to working on the farm. The work was hard, but we only worked eight hours and part of the time we were riding to work on the rail motorcars.

They moved the outfit from time to time when a job was completed. One time I chose to ride along with our headquarter cars. The company wanted someone to stay with the outfit to check for any problems. This was fun as we were hooked onto a freight train for the move. I could go into the kitchen car and eat anything I wanted. Aunt Gertie was a good cook and I put on weight on that job.

My first work for the Western Union was in Indianapolis near the Indy 500 race track. At the time there was some action on the track. They were doing some testing and practice. The linemen up on the poles could see the cars. Since I was on the ground digging holes all I remember was the sound.

Mac Heize was the hard-driving foreman for the gang, but he was fair. If we got to talking too much when we were setting a pole we heard from him in no uncertain terms. From Indianapolis we moved to Ohio to work. Then we went to Michigan on the outskirts of Detroit. At this time I was transferred to a gang working in central Illinois on the Central Illinois Railroad.

Army Air Corp

After thinking it over I decided to volunteer for military duty. I went to the Marine Corp Recruiting station in Indianapolis to take the physical, but to my surprise I failed to pass. They said there was a slight heart murmur, so back home I went.

In October of 1942 I was called to take a physical for the Army. A whole bus load of us from around Leesville went to Fort Benjamin Harrison in Indianapolis for our physical. I passed this one and was asked if I had any objection to serving in the Army Air Corp. (The Air Force was a branch of the Army at that time.)

From Fort Benjamin Harrison we were sent to Jefferson Barracks in Missouri for further processing. It was not long before about eight of us were sent to Kerns Utah Air Base. Kerns was just getting started so the facilities were not all completed yet. There was a kitchen, but no dining hall. We ate from mess kits and washed them in a barrel of boiling hot water. This was a job we had to do for ourselves. Soon they had barracks for us to live in and other buildings were completed as well.

When I got my assignment it was to the 390th Air Force Band. Now this was a surprise to me since I could not play any instruments. They said they'd teach me to play the bugle. The plan was to have a Drum and Bugle Corp to go along with the regular band. Well, I really tried, but I could never get the right sounds to come out of the bugle. Finally, one day the Warrant Officer who was helping us said, "I know what your problem is. You have what is called double lips, so when you blow on the mouth piece the inner part of your lip comes out into the mouthpiece so you don't have any control on the sound."

When I was still trying to learn to play the bugle I became a good friend of Paul Cox. He could play very well as he had played trumpet in high school. Quite often Paul and I were called to reveille at the flag pole. This was an interesting ceremony: Paul would play Reveille as the cannon fired. When it sounded off, up went the flag.

With my bugle lessons over, I was assigned latrine duty. It seemed like my life would often end up with failure: I did poorly in school, was a high school dropout, failed the Marine Corp physical and now I could not even play a simple thing like the bugle. Anyway, I went from latrine duty to CQ duty—that meant being in charge of Quarters for the 390th Band office. This was pretty easy duty, mainly answering the phone and being in the office at night.

One night, one by one some of the Band members came in really sick. I mean sick as though they were dying, vomiting on the floor and frothing at the mouth. I quickly called the hospital to take care of these men. It turned out to be food poisoning and no one died. It was a scary sight for a while.

Another time, after payday, some of the Band members were gambling with dice. I was standing by watching for a few minutes and saw some guy lose all of his monthly pay. When that happened they were broke until the next month (We were paid $21.00 a month in silver dollars). I had just left the room when the M.P. came and caught the guys as they were gambling. This broke up the game for sure.

While I was on CQ duty I worked all night and had the day time free. With this free time I went to the Post Library to study math and a few other things. I thought the math would be needed if I could get reclassified. Then I went to the office for testing to be reclassified. I passed the tests and was assigned to armorer's school. When I was being interviewed for reclassification, the young man I talked to was a Christian. As we were talking, he pointedly asked me if I was a Christian. I hated to admit that I was not.

Before I could go to armorer's school, I needed a doctor to check me out. On a routine physical they thought they detected the heart problem the Marine Corp had found, so the doctor ordered me to the Base Hospital. I was placed in a ward full of men with rheumatic fever. After some time there in the hospital I was told I would be discharged with an Honorable C.D.D, Certificate of Disability Discharge. I was not too happy with this news as I didn't feel sick or weak, but this was the order.

Some of my friends in the band said I was lucky to get out. It is interesting that with my experience in the military I seemed to take a liking to that life, even though I still had the feelings I had in my school days. While in the Army, I was able to cope with my situations with some measure of ease. I realize when I say this that I was not shot at or wounded as many were in the war.

With discharge in hand, I set out for home in August of 1943. I knew that I would be welcomed back home, but was so discouraged that I decided to hitchhike home so it would take more time. It was war time and I was still in uniform, so it was easy to catch a ride. As I moved along, thinking over my recent discharge, the thought came to me that God wanted me out of the service for some reason. I was not a Christian, but I now believe God protects those who are the heirs of Salvation. I marvel as I think back over my life and realize how God has protected me. I could have been killed behind mules or when I had pneumonia or when I fell over the cliff onto the rocks below during the grapevine incident.

Well, this was another failure and another chapter in my journey of life. Traveling on toward home I got a ride with three young men in an old car that was barely limping along. They soon ran out of gas near a ranch house and decided to ask for some gas. I was delegated since I was still in uniform. The people were very friendly and getting ready to go to church. We were given some gas and on we went.

I really wondered who these guys were. They were young men and at that time everybody was working or in the armed services. They didn't comment on where they were going or who they were, but they did me no harm. Soon, however, we were about out of gas again. They saw some heavy equipment about one quarter of a mile from the road. It was Sunday and no one was there. One of the fellows went over to the equipment and came back with some diesel fuel and poured it into the car tank. There must have been a little gas left in the tank to mix with the diesel fuel because it barely ran.

When we came to a hill we all got out and pushed as hard as we could to get up the hill. By then I was getting tired of playing along with the guys, plus it was obvious that the car was on its last legs so I took off and never saw them again. The next ride was with a farmer hauling some grain, as I recall. The old guy was so tired he insisted that I drive, so I crawled in under the steering wheel and took off. The farmer told me where to stop, in some town which I don't remember, then he promptly went to sleep. We arrived safely at his destination and I moved on.

Several rides later I arrived in Saint Louis MO., and still had no trouble getting a ride. Coming out of Vincennes, Indiana on Highway 50 a nice fellow with a tractor trailer stock truck picked me up. I rode with this fellow all the way to Leesville Road. From there it was an easy walk even with a small pack. I was wearing my summer uniform and in my duffel bag I had my winter uniform, my water canteen, mess kit and other items of clothes.

At home again, I was happy to see my parents, but sad that I had to leave some of my friends in the 390th Band. I can still remember the disappointment and regret after all these years. A few days after I got home my dad and I were talking with a person we knew quite well when he said to me, "So they culled you." The way he said it really hurt, as if I was not fit for anything. That remark cut deeply and I remember the hurt, but I had a sense that being out of the Army was the right thing for me.

David (in middle) with Aunt Anita (left) and cousin Bob (right) preparing to gather maple syrup.

David posing on his Harley.

Private First Class, United States Air Force.

Milwaukee Railroad

I arrived home after my time in the Air Force with a bad case of athlete's foot that took some time to heal. After that healed, I started helping my father on the farm. While I enjoyed the work and helping Dad, I thought I should look for another job. Even though I was discharged with a disability, I didn't feel sick.

I went to the Milwaukee Railroad station to ask for work. It was still wartime and they needed all the help they could get. I was hired as a fireman on their steam engines. I rode the passenger train to Faithorn, Illinois to begin working. I trained on the yard engine at first then went on the regular freight runs.

The run I was on went from Faithorn, to Bensonville, Illinois and usually took about eight hours. My job was to keep a good fire going to make steam for power. It was a coal fed engine, and twin mechanical stokers fed the coal into the firebox. These stokers helped to grind the coal, which was then sprayed by air pressure over the hot firebox.

I was careful to watch the water gauge and not let the water get to low and blow up the engine. I would watch the steam gauge and the water gauge and set the stoker to feed in the coal to maintain proper steam. Sometimes on a hard pull I would set the stoker and also shovel coal into the back corners of the firebox to keep up the needed steam. This was not hard physical work since most of the time I was just watching the gauges, but it was enjoyable, plus I had a friendly engineer to work with most of the time.

I remember on one run we had a headwind plus a heavy load, so it took twelve hours to make the run. On another run we pulled into a siding to let a passenger train go by. After waiting for a half hour we got the signal to move. The engineer pulled the lever to apply steam and we moved a few feet then stalled right in the middle of a highway crossing. Cars and trucks were lined up on both sides of the train, but there was nothing we could do until we got up to steam again. We both went to work fueling the fire. It seemed like it took forever to get up to steam and move on. I was careful after that not to let the fire die down. Fortunately I had a good engineer to work with, and in this situation he was very helpful.

When spring came I returned to the farm and never went back to that railroad even though it had been a good experience. I am convinced that God leads in the lives of those he will call to himself. At this time in my life I did not know God and his wonderful love for us.

Operation And Healing

In the spring of 1943, some weeks after returning home, I began to have some weakness and soreness in my feet and hands. This continued to get worse and the doctor I was going to didn't help much. He said I had rheumatic fever. I continued to get worse so decided to see my doctor's partner. The very first time I saw him he said, "I know what your problem is. You not only have rheumatic fever, but you also have a big growth on your thyroid gland. It is choking you and we need to operate and take that growth out." Dr. Ragsdale was his name and he was a fine surgeon. He said the operation was a serious one and could lead to complications or even death.

By then I was so sick I did not care whether I lived or died, in fact I even hoped I would die. We went through with the operation successfully and the growth was removed. Dr. Ragsdale showed dad the thing he took out and Dad said it was as big as a quart canning jar. The growth is commonly called a goiter. Southern Indiana is in what is called the "goiter belt" because there is not enough iodine in the water. With proper treatment for both the goiter and the fever I began to feel better. At this time at least three, and maybe four, young men came around to see me and find out how I was doing. I didn't think I was that popular with the guys, then I realized they wanted to see my young, pretty sister. Donna was popular in high school and fun loving.

One day a friend, Leon Matthews, came over to see me. I thought that was nice of Leon, but I noticed he kept wanting to talk with Donna. Leon had come over to our place in an old Model T Ford car. As we were looking at the old vehicle, Leon asked Donna if she would like to drive it. Ever game to try most anything, she said she would, so Leon showed Donna how to get started. Everything went well at first.

Donna was making circles in our pasture where there was nothing to run into. Then she wanted to stop and didn't know how. Each circle she made she would shout out, "How do I stop?" Leon and I were laughing so hard we couldn't tell her how to stop. Finally Donna ran up a hill and the Model T stopped. Donna took it all in good fun.

As the months went by I continued to feel better and helped Dad on the farm. One day I went to get a wrench to work on a cultivator and started to run. When I did this I realized I was now well and could walk and run without intense pain. I know very definitely that God saw me through. At the time I was not a Christian so didn't know I could go to God for healing. There was no damage to my heart and no troubles with my thyroid—praise the Lord!

To Alaska (1947)

With my health restored, I continued to help Dad on the farm. By this time he had bought a little John Deere model B tractor so we switched from horse power to tractor power. Dad kept one team of horses, Bonnie and Lady, and the big mule, Jim, but Jim was getting old. When he was younger he was a little on the wild side and hard to handle, but he had become very gentle and followed us around like a big, old dog. We discovered when we wanted to do some work with the horses they were so soft and out of shape they could hardly be used. At that time Dad sold the last of the work stock. This ended an era for us—from horses to tractor.

In the early summer of 1947 I decided I would go to Alaska. For most of my life I had an interest in Alaska, Land of the Last Frontier. This seemed like a good time to go, so I went to the Greyhound bus station in Bedford and bought a ticket to Seattle, WA for $38.00. While waiting in Seattle and trying to decide what to do next, I thought of enlisting in the Army again. As I talked to an Army recruiter it came to me that this was not a good idea. Next I went to an Employment Office and found that a gold mining company was hiring men to work in their operation in Alaska. This sounded good, so I soon found myself bound for Alaska in a DC3 airplane. I landed in Juneau then went onto Fairbanks. A fellow from the FE Co. met us at the airport with a flatbed truck and took us to the mine.

The mine was located on Ester Creek not too far from Fairbanks. I was put to work on the pipeline carrying water to the mining operation. It took a lot of water for the operation, which was to thaw the frozen dirt down to bedrock where the gold was. In some places they used a hydraulic water system which was a strong powerful stream of water coming from a three or four inch nozzle, which slowly thawed the frozen dirt.

In other places steam thawing was used. Also, a large drag line was used to scoop off the loose material ahead of the dredge. The dredge was a large boat-like affair floating on a man-made pond. The gold-bearing gravel was scooped up by large steel buckets on a conveyor then dumped in the dredge. There the gravel was washed down through a series of sluice boxes and finally into the last box where the gold settled out. The tailings went out the back.

I was called on several times to help in the clean-up. This was when the gold was taken from the dredge to be processed elsewhere. I remember carrying buckets of gold off the dredge. This gold mining was all very interesting—the huge electric powered drag line that walked, the dredge, the steam thawing and the huge water-powered hoses shooting the water up against the frozen dirt. There were many prehistoric bones, tusks, teeth and skulls washed out during this process. I picked up a broken tusk and a huge tooth which was probably from a mammoth. Most of the better bones were picked up by people from the University or a museum. All my Alaska souvenirs were later stolen from the farm house in Indiana along with all the Indian arrow heads I had collected over the years on the farm.

The mine crew was housed in a big building with a kitchen and dining hall on the first floor and sleeping rooms upstairs. Each room was prepared for two people. My roommate was a tall fellow who was the oiler on the drag line. He was a friendly, interesting guy. A lot of men working there were drifters going from job to job looking for adventure. Some had served in World War II. Others were young men working to make money for college. One of the men in the next room was an ex-marine who had guarded American Embassies around the world. I liked to hear tales about jobs they had and other experiences. One time I overheard a conversation about me. One said to the other, "You can take the boy out of the country, but you can't take the country out of the boy." That didn't insult me at all; I like the country. All in all, I got along well with the men I worked with there. I remember one evening after work, my roommate and the ex-marine got to throwing knives at the wall. Maybe they were trying to impress me, I don't know. Anyway it was not too good for the wall.

It was a good experience to work there. We worked 12 ½ hours a day seven days a week, which didn't leave much chance to see the country. One time I heard about an old timer living nearby, named Moose John. I was told he was friendly, so I walked to his cabin. The old fellow lived all alone in his tipsy log cabin which was very neat and clean. It was an adventure for me to be in Alaska. I was not attacked by bears nor run over by a moose or threatened by an outlaw with a gun. Some of the men working there at that time may have been a little on the rough side, but I never felt threatened by anyone.

Back To Indiana

After my summer in Alaska, I returned home and started attending a farm school at Shawswick High School, taught by Mr. Rush Armstrong. Rush was a good teacher, a graduate of Purdue University. The subjects taught were of practical value for a farmer: bookkeeping, how to prepare a record system for expense, depreciation, inventory, income, soil preparation, planting, tilling, harvesting, marketing, welding, carpentry, mechanics, etc. This was very helpful.

We were encouraged to do individual home projects such as welding a piece of equipment for the farm or building something. Those projects were designed to gain experience with the tools needed for the project and work on the farm itself. We also made trips to farms to see demonstrations of haying equipment operated by the Purdue Experiment Station, forestry practices and land control, such as terracing and waterway design to control flooding. There was some book work involved, but no college credit was given. I received a certificate saying I had completed 3½ years of classes. I was happy to receive this because it showed I had completed a course of study that was helpful to the farm.

Farming was what I liked to do, so Dad and I rented a few more acres. Then in 1948 I bought a new John Deere tractor, a cultivator, corn planter and a real good used 12A John Deere Combine. This gave me a good basic set of machinery to operate with. That same year a farm nearby became available for rent. I visited the owner and ended up renting the farm. This gave us almost more acres than we could handle and I regretted not buying a bigger tractor. By working long hours and hiring another young fellow, John Bob Sherfick, we were able to get the crops planted.

Those were busy days, with going to night school and working long hours. I remember hanging at least three five-gallon gas cans on the tractor and working until I was out of gas. During the heat of the day I would get so sleepy that it's a wonder I didn't fall off and kill myself.

One time I did have an accident with the older John Deere tractor that we had. I was going to work and came to the gate at the far end of the pasture, north of the house. As I started through the gate our flock of sheep wanted to go through also. As I looked back trying to stop the sheep, the front wheel went over the bank and I could not keep it from going down into the creek below, onto the solid rock bottom.

As it was going over, I bailed off the back and the sheep got out also. I received a few bruises, nothing serious, but the tractor sure looked bad. It had landed on the front wheel, flipped upside down and back again. The front wheels, steering wheel and column were broken, the exhaust pipe was badly bent and one rear tire went flat. I felt sick about this and wondered what to say to Dad.

As usual, Dad took the news calmly and said that we'd have to get the tractor out of the creek so it could be repaired. As I was thinking of how that could be done, Dad had a practical solution. We rounded up the two horses we had left. Old Jim was not much use, but we hitched them to a wagon and managed to get the tractor up and out of the creek and to the barn. Dad ordered some parts from the dealer in Bedford to fix the broken tractor. The mechanic from John Deere, Bruce Butler, came out to the farm to help in the repair job. Bruce just laughed when he saw the tractor. Personally, I didn't think it was funny. I marvel at Dad's patience with me and my mistakes. I knew he was very disappointed, but he just went to work to fix the damage. After it was repaired we used it until we sold it at a farm sale later.

One day I was in Indianapolis and came upon a Harley Davidson motorcycle dealership. For some reason I had wanted a motorcycle so I went in to look. I ended up buying a Harley 45. Since I had never ridden a motorcycle before, the dealer took me out of the city and I took it from there. I had no trouble getting home.

I soon got tired of just riding around with no purpose, and besides I was busy with the farm. I did ride it to the night school some of the time. One night on the way home from school I ran into a ridge of gravel the county grader had left in the center of the road. This really threw me and I landed on the gravel road with the motorcycle lying on its side and the motor still running. I had some scratches and bruises, but the motorcycle seemed to be okay, so I rode on home. Sometime after that I sold the motorcycle to John Bob Sherfick. That ended my experience with motorcycles.

As I write about this time in my life—the 3½ years between the fall of 1947 to spring of 1951—it doesn't seem all that interesting and exciting. It was a time of hard work, long hours, night school and growing the farm enterprise. My main focus was growing hogs for market. Most of the corn I grew I fed to the hogs, which at that time were a good business. I got to know men in the farm school though I wasn't close friends with anyone. Those were pretty good years for us. Mother and Dad were in good health. Dad had a laying hen enterprise, up to 1,000 laying hens, which gave several cases of eggs to sell each week. This allowed my parents to improve the house and their lifestyle. He added a room and bathroom to the house. Dad and I bought a dependable used 1946 Plymouth sedan. The old 38 Dodge was sold after many years of service.

I really enjoyed what I was doing. I could hardly wait for Monday morning to come so I could go to work. Only the necessary work was done on Sunday. After going to Sunday school and church each Sunday growing up, I didn't attend very much. The Bishop would harangue the small congregation because they had not come up with their quota of money for the quarter. Not being a Christian at the time I stayed away. Mother and Dad continued to go for a while then went to another church. Mother was a born again believer and knew she was. She was saved at age 19 at an evangelistic meeting. Dad accepted the Lord later in life. Not going to church left me with very little contact with other people since I never went anywhere unless I had to.

Crowded To Christ

One day in the spring of 1951, I went to the barn to begin work as usual. In the barn-lot as I checked on the livestock and just looked around, the thought came to me that what I had accomplished so far had not brought the joy and happiness that I thought it would. At that point I became very discouraged and confused. God was speaking to me about material things and beginning the process of crowding me to Himself, but I did not know this at the time. I was on a downward course emotionally, not knowing what to do or where to turn. Some days I felt so bad I would burst into tears. I didn't know God's word at the time, but in Mark 8:36 it asks, "What good is it for a man to gain the whole world, yet forfeit his soul?" At the time I didn't understand why these accomplishments didn't satisfy. I had worked hard to get where I was, with good equipment all paid for and money in the bank.

About this time my lovely sister married Dr. Philip Hennessee and they took note that I was not doing so well. Phil suggested I go see a psychologist, a professor at Indiana University that he knew. I thought, "What can I lose?", so I went to see the "shrink". He was a nice guy and friendly. He wanted me to do most of the talking and I was not used to spilling my innermost thoughts to a stranger. Talking to him did ease the pressure somewhat, but it was no cure. I remember he asked me if I had had a religious experience. Well I could honestly say that I hadn't. I believe I went for three sessions, maybe four at the most.

At this time the thought came to me that maybe I should go back to Alaska. Perhaps things would be better up there. But the truth is we cannot run away from our problems. I was thinking also that I was 29 years old and still at home with my parents and maybe I should get away for a while. God in His great mercy and loving kindness was slowly crowding me to Himself. Of course at the time I never had any thought that this was God's doing.

I talked to Mother and Dad about this idea. They knew I was having problems and had no idea what to do about them. Their thought was that if that is what I wanted to do it was all right with them. As it turned out it was good for all of us. I am so thankful for godly parents. They stayed with me all the way.

With the decision made to go back to Alaska, I went to Bedford to the Greyhound bus station and asked the ticket agent for a ticket from Bedford to Fairbanks, Alaska. I don't think the man had ever been asked for a ticket like that before. He hesitated a few seconds then said he would have to contact the head office in Cincinnati, Ohio. I said that was okay with me as I had to make a few preparations. Soon I received word that Greyhound had tickets for Alaska. With that news I packed one suitcase for the trip and Mother and Dad took me to the bus station. I was leaving home not knowing what lay ahead.

It was to be over three years before I got back. Some relations I never saw again. Uncle Ross, Aunt Gertie and Uncle Ralph waved to me as we passed their homes. Arriving at the bus station, the agent wanted to call a reporter from the newspaper for an interview and pictures. I vetoed that idea quickly because I just didn't feel like going through an interview. I remember the ticket, when unfolded, was about as long as I was tall. Soon the bus arrived and I was on my way by bus to Alaska, but I was not a happy camper. It was with a sad, heavy heart that I left my parents and the farm—the only occupation that I knew and loved to do. Good decision or bad decision, I was on my way to the great state of Alaska. God, however unknown to me at the time, was crowding me ever closer to Himself. I am convinced that God seeks us first before we respond to His call. John 15:16 tells us "You did not choose me, but I chose you…"

The bus traveled through Indiana and into Illinois and I well remember a stop somewhere in Illinois where we could get off to get something to eat. I was not one bit hungry. As I walked outside the restaurant I could see the black, rich soil of northern Illinois. This caused me to think, "What am I doing here, leaving parents and the farm I love." The thought came to me of just going back home and forgetting the whole business of going to Alaska, but when the bus left I was on board, bound for points north. We crossed into Canada without any problems and went to Winnipeg, Manitoba. At that point the bus passengers were informed we would have to ride a passenger train because late April break-up time had begun, which made the roads soft. I always liked train travel so it was no problem to ride the train from Winnipeg to Calgary, Alberta.

At Calgary we boarded another bus to continue the journey. We angled northwest from Edmonton, around Slave Lake then on to Dawson Creek, where the Alaska Highway begins. We had some time to wait until the next bus left, so I started to look the town over. It wasn't a very big place, but nevertheless an historic town. In walking around I came upon a John Deere Farm equipment dealer. This was interesting to me, so I walked in to see their line of equipment, since nearly all my equipment was John Deere. I explained to him that I was a farmer from Indiana on my way to Alaska. I could see that there was some good looking farm land in the Dawson Creek area. The thought came to me that maybe I should stay in this area and look for some land. But I still had some of that long ticket left, so when the bus pulled out I was once again on board, traveling up the Alaska Highway.

By now I was beginning to take more interest in the country, the road, which was 1200 miles of gravel, and the little settlements along the highway. There was no night travel on the Alaskan highway so we stayed overnight in what were once construction camps. After Dawson Creek there was Fort Nelson, then Watson Lake, and Whitehorse on the Yukon River.

Some of the settlements had been occupied for many years. From Whitehorse we traveled to Kluane Lake, Beaver Creek and then through customs at the U.S. border, into Alaska. I couldn't see that it looked much different in Alaska than the Yukon Territory I had just left. At Tok we were informed a bridge was out on the highway and we would have to make a long detour down the Tok Cut-off to where it met the Richardson Highway. It was on the Tok Cut-off that I first saw Alaska Native Indians. I was fascinated by their dress and speech. At

Gakona we stayed the night in the historic Gakona Lodge. From there we traveled to the Richardson and drove north until it joined the Alaska Highway at Delta Junction, then went on to Fairbanks. Arriving in Fairbanks the bus company had made reservations for me to stay in downtown Fairbanks. The Greyhound Bus Company had done a good job in getting me to my destination safely. The trip took eleven days.

It was a good trip and I had seen a lot of God's creation, from the rich mid-western states of Illinois, Wisconsin, and Minnesota, the wide prairie-land of Manitoba, Saskatchewan, and Alberta, to the mountains of British Columbia and Yukon Territory. At the time of this trip I was not thinking of God as the Creator. As I write this looking back, I can thank God for His creation. Psalm 104:24 says, "How many are your works, O Lord! In wisdom you made them all; the earth is full of your creatures."

Now that I was in Fairbanks I needed to decide what to do. I did not seek employment or go out to the FE Gold Mine, but rather just seemed to put in time doing nothing. During a conversation with another man at the hotel I heard there was work to be had in Anchorage. Then he mentioned that land was open for homesteading on the Kenai Peninsula. As I was thinking over what this fellow had told me, I decided to go see what Anchorage looked like, since I had never been there before. God was still moving me to Himself.

By this time I was tired of bus travel so I went to the airport and caught a flight to Anchorage, then took a taxi to a downtown hotel. At the time I didn't know where else to go since I was new to the town and didn't know one person there. I got settled in a room in a hotel on Fourth Avenue, then decided to take a walk around the place to see what kind of a burg it was. In May 1951, Fourth Avenue had plenty of bars. I know because later I made deliveries to many of them. I had barely started on my walk when two GI's came along and handed me a little card announcing Gospel meetings at Carpenter's Hall. The speaker was to be Dr. Bob Jones Sr. Sometime in the past I had heard that name but didn't know anything about him. Carpenter's Hall was only a few blocks from where I was staying, so I decided to go hear this well-known preacher just to put in time.

I went to the meeting and sat on a folding chair near the back of the room. And what a meeting it was! God was waiting to meet me there and tell me that I was lost forever if I did not ask the Lord Jesus Christ to save me and forgive me of my sins. Dr. Bob Jones Sr. used Proverbs 22:6 as his text: "Train up a child in the way he should go and when he is old he will not depart from it." God the Holy Spirit used that verse to speak to me in a way that I had never experienced before. In a way it was both wonderful and terrifying—the thought of spending eternity in hell, the pain of torment, the blackness of darkness forever and worse than that even was the separation from the Holy and Righteous God, the God of Light in whom there is no darkness at all.

I am absolutely convinced that the way God spoke to me that night at Carpenter's Hall was a vision from God Himself. There was the picture of the awful, terrible, painful darkness of hell—such darkness that it was hard to imagine and the utterly absolute hopelessness of eternity and never getting out to freedom. This experience was so overwhelming that I was practically oblivious to what was going on around me. The only scripture I remember Dr. Bob spoke about was Prov. 22:6, "Train up a child..." Then there was a bright white light and from this brilliant light came such a sense of God's presence and love that it was almost overwhelming. This loving kindness just drew me to want to know and obey Him. Like I said earlier, the worst possible thing, even worse than hell itself, was to be separated from this God of light, glory and loving kindness.

This experience and vision from God is very difficult to adequately express in words. The wonder of it all still amazes me even to this day. This is the truth and I am not lying or dreaming about the experience. I give God all the praise and glory because it was His doing from start to finish. I am so thankful to God for His grace and mercy to this most unworthy sinner. Titus 3:5 says "He saved us, not because of righteous things we had done, but because of his mercy."

There was no doubt in my mind that this God of Light was speaking to me and calling me to Himself. I Corinthians 1:9 tells us that God calls people—"God, who has called you into fellowship, with his Son Jesus Christ our Lord, is faithful." By the end of the meeting I knew

I needed to talk to whoever was up front. So up front I went and sat down on a chair to talk with someone. As I went to the front, I didn't care who saw me or what they thought. Of course no one but God knew me anyway.

I ended up going two nights to the meetings. One time I talked with Rev. Walkup. Then two young men came over to talk with me. They explained the plan of salvation and that I needed to ask forgiveness and for God to cleanse me from all my sin. I knew beyond a doubt I was a sinner and not going the right way, God's Way. So I accepted the free gift of salvation that night. "For by grace you have been saved, through faith—and this not from yourselves, it is the gift of God" (Ephesians 2:8-9).

The two young men who came to talk with me were Johnny Gillespie and Art Kimble. They were very friendly and invited me to go to their church. Not knowing where else to attend church, I went to the little log church on Fourth Avenue, called the Church of the Open Door. It turned out the church was near where I was staying and John Gillespie was the pastor, a man who became a lifelong friend.

As I think now about that time, up until the night I accepted Christ as my Savior I can see that God was leading me, calling me, ever crowding me to Himself, especially starting with the time on the farm when I was reminded that material things do not in and of themselves bring happiness. Other times included the visits with the professor, the deep depression, the trip to Alaska by bus, lingering in Fairbanks and then on to Anchorage by plane. The timing was practically down to the minute to get me all the way to Anchorage on the right day, the right afternoon and the right minute for the GI's to meet me there on the sidewalk!

Trusting the Lord Jesus Christ as my Savior and Lord was the most important, wonderful and exciting thing that happened in all my life. This was a major turning point. I turned from a life of defeat, depression and despair to a life of hope.

New Life In Christ

2 Corinthians 5:17 says, "Therefore if any man be in Christ he is a new creation, old things are passed away, behold all things have become new." When I started to read my Bible soon after making the decision to accept the Lord Jesus Christ as my Savior, 2 Corinthians 5:17 was the first verse that God used to speak to me. This was exciting because I realized something had happened in my life, my heart, and I was a new creation in Christ Jesus. God the Holy Spirit had come to dwell in my heart.

This gave me a real desire to read the Bible. Mother had insisted that I take a Bible on my travels, so I had packed my little New Testament that I had while in the Army. I began reading the New Testament, then purchased a complete Bible. I started attending the Church of the Open Door. The first day I was in Anchorage I had walked by this log building whose sign said "Church of the Open Door" and asked myself, "What kind of a denomination is this?" I had never heard of a church by that name. As I walked by I never gave a thought that I would be attending there. The people were so friendly—there were lots of children, young people and military personnel.

Everything seemed so new. The old hymns took on new meaning. In no time I had a church full of friends. I can remember one Sunday, without thinking about what I was doing, I sat almost on the front seat. For me to sit up front was a new thing. That was another indication that things really were different with me. I soon learned to listen very carefully to Johnny's preaching. I don't think I had ever heard Biblical teaching and preaching like this before. The teachers, such as Floyd Gilman and Marvin Webber, were very good also. It didn't take long before I wanted to be in church for every service. This was truly an exciting time for me—a new church and making new friends.

41

Alaska Railroad & Air Transport Associates

I soon got a job with the Alaska Railroad on the T&T gang—Telephone & Telegraph. This was the same kind of work that I had done on the New York Central Railroad. I liked railroad work. The first job was around Turnagain Arm south of Anchorage. A snow slide had wiped out about 300 yards of line. Our job was to string temporary wire over the hard packed snow to restore service. This was very interesting to me as it was May and warm but we were walking over snow stringing the wire. The mountains and water of Turnagain Arm were beautiful and made me think of God, the Creator. Pretty soon we moved down the tracks to Moose Pass. While there we could hear snow slides coming off the mountains and it sounded just like thunder. This was an amazing sight and sound. We also worked at Peter's Creek and then went up to Denali Park.

While we were in the Peter's Creek-Birchwood area our gang got a truck for the workers. The foreman appointed me to get the truck, so I went to the railroad yards and picked up the truck, an Army 6X6. After that I was a truck driver instead of a hole-digger. About this time I began to realize that if I stayed with the job I would not be able to get to church very much. Then the foreman informed me the gang was getting a dozer with a hole-digger on the back. The job was looking better all the time, yet I felt the need to attend church on a regular basis.

At that time, in 1951, the Alaska Communication System was under the control of the Army Signal Corp., so half or more of the T&T gang were military. We all worked together, but the GI's had their own rail car accommodations. I remember the Army supply would bring out different things to entertain the troops. They had plenty of movies and sometimes I would watch for a few minutes, but I could never sit through a whole movie. Some GI's asked me one day what I did for fun. They didn't think going to church was much fun. Their idea of fun was going into Anchorage and getting drunk, coming back sick as a dog, and then having to recover from all the partying. That didn't look like fun to me.

Despite our differences we got along very well. They were not making fun of me, but they just didn't understand what I got out of life. One young man came up to me one day to talk. He told me he would like to have what I had. At the time I didn't know just how to answer him. It hurts to know that I failed to tell him about Jesus. I have prayed for him many times.

One evening we were on a siding at Birchwood when I felt a good jolt. At first I thought an engine had hooked onto the rail cars to move the outfit to another location. Looking out the window I could see the slender birch trees waving, and I realized it was an earthquake. That was my first earthquake in Alaska.

One time we were working in the Talkeetna area when we noticed a very small black bear. Two of the guys put on heavy leather gloves and caught the little fellow and brought the bear inside. It got loose and ran into the dining area and into the kitchen and hid behind the cook stove. They finally caught the little guy again and turned him loose.

While working with the men on the T&T gang I had a real sense that the Lord was with me all the time in whatever I did. I began to develop more confidence in work and with people. I distinctly remember playing softball with the GI's and doing very well. This had to be the Lord. But at the same time I still struggled with insecurity and wondered if I was really saved. Then I would realize unbelief is sin so I had to confess my sin and pray to God to help my unbelief just as the father in Mark 9:24 did. God is so patient with us. I wanted to live my life in obedience to the Lord and his commandments. With all my doubts and fears I never lost hope that I could have a closer walk with the Lord. I knew my life was changing and God was using His Word to speak to me. This was a real growing time for me.

At that time I struggled over the question of whether or not I should stay in Anchorage or go back to the farm. I really wanted to go back where I came from and tell my family and friends about the Lord and what had happened to me. I talked to friends like Johnny Gillespie, Pop Parmenter and Floyd Gilman. They all told me why I shouldn't go back there, with all the problems on the farm. I thought at the time, sure there are problems with farming, but I had been doing it successfully.

Sensing the need to be in church more, I left the job with the railroad and went back to Anchorage. I did not like Anchorage then or now. The only reason I went back was so I could get to church more. I felt at that time I needed the teaching and instruction that Johnny was giving us. I was so ignorant of the Bible, even with going to Sunday school and church most of my life.

I would read and read the Bible and it was so interesting. One day I was reading in the New Testament and came to I John. I had never heard of I John before. Reading it helped me to understand that we can know that we are saved. I even counted the number of times the word "know" is mentioned. I John 5:13 says, "I write these things to you who believe in the name of the Son of God so that you may *know* that you have eternal life." My godly mother also helped me in the matter of knowing if I was saved or not. She wrote, telling me in no uncertain words that I needed to believe and trust God's Word. I surely took her counsel to heart. Thank God for praying mothers who love their children.

In Anchorage I met one of the guys I had worked with on the railroad job. He was working for Air Transport Associates—ATA. This airline hauled mostly freight to Alaska. Dick DeJong helped me get a job with this airline. Our job was unloading the planes early in the morning, and then driving a truck around town delivering the freight. I soon learned where the businesses were so it was not a difficult job. The airline hauled all kinds of stuff to Alaska like fresh produce, groceries, dry goods, auto parts, clothing, and even live animals. One time I opened the plane door and there was a big Doberman dog on top of everything. Fortunately he was not vicious.

We delivered a lot of products to the bars along Fourth Avenue. I can say that I frequented all the bars on Fourth Avenue! I always went in the dingy back doors and did not linger in those establishments. The 1964 earthquake wiped out most of those bars. Another business I went to quite often was Betty Farris Apparel. There I had to go in the front door with the goods. Those women had to examine each dress and every item while I stood there through the whole process. Finally, when they had looked at and examined each dress, I could escape.

The airline had two trucks for the deliveries. One was a cab-over with a closed box. The other was smaller and the box didn't have any door on the back. I usually drove the larger truck with the better back door. One day for some reason I got the small truck with no back doors. That day we had a full load and my truck was stacked full. When I took off I lost a few items out the back. Some we picked up, but some were lost. I got chewed out pretty good for that one. Even with that happening I had a good record with ATA. Sometimes if there was not much work to do, the mechanics would ask me to help work on the plane. After freight was off the plane, we would clean up the floor, lock the seats in place, and then they would haul passengers back to Seattle.

It was also at this time that I got acquainted with some of the young people at church. Most were college kids up for the summer to get work to help them through school. Leo Powell was one, Barney Furman, who was in Alaska as a missionary, another. These fellows were staying in the church so I was invited to join them there. This was great as I liked to be in the church. There was always something of interest going on. Missionaries would come by, like Alan Franz, missionary pilot, Everett Bachelder with his pack dog, Pinky, and Indian Chief, Douglas Billam, from Copper Center.

This was a special time for me, staying at the church with the fellows and making new friends. Ernie Lucia, Preston Harrison and I were becoming good friends. Even though I was a little older than most of the young people, I thought they knew it all because they had gone to Bob Jones University. Another fellow about my age was Dick Gotting, from Sweden. That fall all the students went back to college, so Dick and I went to room with Art and Glennie Kimball.

While I was still working for ATA and staying with Art and Glennie the Lord spoke to me about some language I was using—like

Gee, Geez and other minced oaths and sometimes more. I am ashamed to admit that at the time I did take God's name in vain. When I would say a wrong word it was like a bad taste in my mouth. Finally I caught on that the Lord did not want me to take His name in vain. The third commandment tells us this (Exodus 20:7). God taught me to clean up my speech. This was a very important lesson for me and I never forgot it. I seem to be a slow learner and no doubt there are other things in my life that with God's help and His conviction need to be corrected. Praise the Lord He loves us enough to correct us. We are commanded to be holy because God is holy (I Peter 1:15-16). That experience was another proof that I was saved because God disciplines those He loves. (Hebrews 12:6-13)

The year of 1951 was certainly a year of change for me and important things were happening around the world as well. I was a new creation in Christ and had a new church and new friends. Johnny Gillespie and others had started a Bible camp a few years earlier that was expanding. He was also instrumental in organizing Alaska Missions to bring the good news of Jesus Christ to Alaska. The Korean War was in full battle. I remember so well after World War II was over I really thought that it was a war to end all wars. How mistaken I was. All in all it was an exciting time in my life. What a great God we serve!

The Trucking Business

In the fall of 1951, Dick DeJong, my friend from Alaska Railroad days and ATA, decided we should go into the trucking business. After talking to a salesman at Alaska Sales and Service, we chose a new GMC 620 single axle tractor which was in Seattle, and a good used trailer for hauling freight. The salesman, Lucky, said he would go with us to Seattle.

Dick talked ATA into giving us a free flight to Seattle. When we got there Lucky had a hotel room for us. That evening, Lucky came to our room with two very attractive young women. He and a friend of his had rounded up these two women and they were going out on the town. I knew that Lucky had a wife back home in Anchorage, but he was here and going to have a "good time". That is the way many in the world live. It's pleasure for the moment. Dick and I were not invited to go along and I would not have gone anyway.

Lucky was true to his word and helped us find a flat-bed trailer. With a little work it was ready to go. At this time I broke out with small boils. Finally I went to a doctor in Seattle for help. The doctor gave me a shot of penicillin, but it turned out I was allergic to penicillin. It cured the boils, but I broke out with a severe rash all over my back and seat, more painful than the boils. We traveled to Great Falls, Montana, where I went to another doctor for help. With more medication I started to get better. Even so I was in misery for about three more days.

At Great Falls we got a load to haul to Eielson Air Base near Fairbanks. This was December 1951, and we were starting a trip up the Alaska Highway in the dead of winter. Fortunately Dick had some experience driving a tractor trailer as I had none. Before we left Seattle we had met up with Dick's father at a railroad yard. He had brought up a carload of dairy cattle from California. From his father Dick had gotten money for his half of the truck. What I didn't know at the time was that after he paid Lucky the money, Dick was broke again.

By the time we got to Great Falls I realized I would need some more money to get us up the highway to Alaska. So I went to a bank there and had them wire some money from my bank in Anchorage. We took turns driving through the Prairie Provinces where it was pretty good highway. There were a few miles of pure ice on the highway. We were moving pretty good until we got into the mountains. The highway was hard packed snow which was better than the dusty gravel road in the summer.

On the steeper hills we had to put on chains. We had dual chains and we got pretty good at putting on the iron. This was another adventure, traveling up the Alaska Highway in December! This vast country was all coated in its winter covering. The North Country has its beauty and attraction even in the winter. The lakes were all frozen over. That time of the year meant we were in the shortest daylight hours of the year and so we drove in the dark part of the time. At night we would get a room at one of the roadhouses.

I'm sure I was not the best companion for Dick. I remember I would fall silent, deep in thought, thinking over the turn of events of the past five months and how God had spoken to me to call me to Him. I so desperately wanted to follow the Lord and yet at times I wondered if I was really saved or not. At that time my emotions did not feel like I thought a Christian should feel. What does it feel like to be a Christian? Then I realized God had spoken to me in a powerful way by His Word, the Bible. He gave me friends, in fact a whole new life and a new hope. God is a God of Hope (Romans 15:13). I seemed always to be an introvert looking inside instead of upward to the One who gave us life and hope. Dick would ask me what I was thinking about and that would rouse me out of my negative thinking patterns.

We moved along pretty well considering winter conditions. There was one time when I was driving that we came to a steep downhill section. I believe we had just crossed the summit. Anyway, going down this steep hill I put the trailer brakes on a little too much and caused the trailer to slide into a ditch. It was a shallow ditch and it came right out. We got down to a stopping place to see what damage had been done. There was a busted tire and that was all we could see. We had a couple of spares so we put one on and off we went. It could have been much worse. We didn't lose the load and the trailer went into the ditch next to a hill instead of over the edge on the other side where there was a drop of several hundred feet. Praise the Lord!

Another time we powered out going up a hill near Fort Nelson. A fuel truck pulled in front of us and we hooked on and were helped up. At one of the roadhouse stops we made, there was a young woman who needed a ride to another roadhouse, so we said she could ride with us and she joined us for about 150 miles. I can't remember that she talked very much. I don't think she smelled very good, but maybe it was me. By then we had not had baths for some time. Anyway we got her to the right place.

When we got to Whitehorse, Yukon Territory, Dick wanted the carburetor checked. He was a better mechanic than I was. We got that taken care of and moved on. Somewhere up the line we came upon a young couple pulling a two wheeled trailer with an older car. We stopped to check on them. They were from the lower 48 and on their way to Alaska. We decided to put their trailer on the back of our trailer. I don't remember how we got the trailer up there, but we did. We must have gone to the nearest roadhouse for a loading ramp. The young couple had an infant with them. The car was so full there was barely enough room to sit. They followed along behind us until we got to Tok. They were going to Anchorage and we had to deliver the freight to Eielson in Fairbanks.

After Eielson we went back to Anchorage and leased the truck to BMR Trucking. We drove our truck for them, hauling freight from Anchorage to Fairbanks. One trip I remember because of the cold. We couldn't keep warm in the truck. At Tok it was so cold I could hardly turn the steering wheel. We got to Dot Lake and decided to stay there for the night. They said it was 63 degrees below zero and it sure felt cold. We used a space heater to warm up the engine so the truck would start. We arrived in Fairbanks where it had warmed up to about

50 below. I remember turning a corner in downtown Fairbanks and a brake line to the trailer broke, locking up the wheels. Dick jumped out and released the brake so we could move. We unloaded and returned to Anchorage.

I began to think about being in business with an unbeliever. Dick said he went to the Dutch Reformed Church, but I could see some things that caused concern. I read in the Bible that we are not to be unequally yoked with unbelievers. (II Corinthians 6:14) Sometime in early 1952 Dick asked if I would sell my half of the business. I agreed, so that ended my career in the trucking business. We parted friends and I would see Dick from time to time. We just didn't see eye to eye on some things. I think it was the right thing to do for both of us.

Anchorage (1951-1952)

Among the many friends I got acquainted with were Maver and Carmen Roth. They came to Alaska the same year as I did, as missionaries. After Alaska Missions was formed Maver was called to be the Mission carpenter and I helped him on a few projects. This included work on the mission house in Cantwell where Pauline Smith was serving. While there I came down with the mumps. I was so sick that I could not work or travel. Pauline was so nice; she stayed at a neighbor's house during the night and came to help me through the day. Finally I got strength enough to board the train and go back to Anchorage.

About this time the Mission was interested in establishing a ministry in the Indian settlement of Tyonek. Maver put together a complete house, pre-cut and ready to be put up, including kitchen equipment, floor covering, everything they needed. A fellow by the name of Calhoun was contracted to barge the house material across Cook Inlet to Tyonek with his old World War II landing barge. We loaded everything on board and took off. Maver, Carmen, Dean Thimson and I were on the craft. All went well until the barge got stuck on a sand bar out in the Cook Inlet. Soon we were high and dry on a sand bar. Calhoun called for help and the Air Force 10th Rescue sent out a helicopter to take us back to land.

The concern was that when the tide came in it would damage the barge. The tide in Cook Inlet is the second highest in the world. The barge did sustain minor damage and was towed back to Anchorage. We unloaded all the materials to be used for other projects. Apparently it was not the Lord's timing for a ministry in the village of Tyonek.

This was an exciting time with my new friends in Christ: Ernie Lucia, Preston Harrison, Maver and Carmen and many others. I got acquainted with another great fellow by the name of John Nelson. John had lived in Alaska a good number of years and then moved to Washington State to work on an apple orchard. One way to market his apples was using apple vending machines. He placed some at Elmendorf Air Force Base and Fort Richardson. I helped John supply the apple vending machines. I had purchased a good used Chevy pickup truck so I could haul some of the apples to the bases. When John went to Washington he sent up a man to take care of the business. I helped Al Opp for some time.

One day I was with John Nelson out on Elmendorf Air Force base taking care of the machine. John knew a friend in the personnel office on the base who told me they needed a man to take the position of receiving and shipping clerk in a huge warehouse. Suddenly I found myself working for the US Air Force as a warehouseman—in a supervisor position. This was a new page in my life. New housing was being built on the base so I moved into one of three brand new apartments. It was a good job and a good place to stay. There were ten men on my crew and they seemed to know what to do. Mainly I signed paperwork for everything that came through the warehouse. The men under me were all military GI's, and some were Christians.

Two friends that attended Church of the Open Door also lived on base so I would take them to church using my pickup. There was Mr. Hack, a wonderful man, and a young lady, Marie Haldtrust. Marie was a very nice young person, but at that time in my life I was just enjoying being single so didn't pay much attention to her. After about two years with the Air Force I changed jobs. I just didn't think I wanted to spend the rest of my working life in that position.

Margaret

At one time I stayed with my good friend Ernie Lucia in his little trailer. Then Ernie went back east and came back with a wife so out I went. This got me to thinking, that here I was in my thirties and no girlfriend or wife.

For some time I had taken on the job of janitor for the church. I really enjoyed doing this just to be of help and be where the action was. I know I pestered Johnny more than I should have. One day as I was cleaning the floor in the church Margaret Broady came by on crutches, her leg in a cast. The Lord said to me, "Someone needs to take care of her". I immediately said, "Not me, Lord. It looks like she is doing very well on her own." I hardly knew her, though I would often see her at church. After thinking this over for some time I decided to ask if Margaret would go with me to a Youth for Christ meeting. I had been going to their meetings down at Carpenter's Hall where the Lord first met me and called me to Himself.

I had never dated a young woman and had no close women friends. With a great deal of apprehension I approached her door one evening to ask it she would go with me. I remember thinking I didn't know if I would feel worse if she turned me down or accepted my invitation. Anyway, Margaret said she would go with me.

At that time Margaret was staying with another single lady, Sylvia Bray. They told me afterwards that they were not sure if I was asking Margaret or Sylvia. I soon found that Margaret was a very nice person and was easy to talk with. We had much in common, both saved in our twenties and both loved the Lord. Through our more than 50 years together we would often talk about how good God was to call us to Himself.

Margaret Genevieve Broady was born in Johnson, Nebraska on May 4, 1919 to Frank and Dot Broady. Her twin sister, Marian, was born an hour before her, and their younger sister Betty was born five years later. Following a move to southern California when the twins were babies, Margaret grew up in San Dimas, at that time an area of citrus groves. The Depression years were hard on the family. Their father was out of work for a time and the girls helped the family however they could with jobs such as babysitting. Marian and Margaret graduated from Bonita Union High School in LaVerne, and then earned their associate of arts degrees from Chaffey Junior College in 1939.

The family had attended a Christian church during their growing up years but it wasn't until their early twenties that both Margaret and Marian were saved. After that they attended the Bible Institute of Los Angeles where they joined the Alaska prayer team. Through that group they met Johnny Gillespie and Don Stump, missionaries in Alaska. Margaret thoroughly enjoyed her college years and soaked up the Bible teaching. She earned her way through school by various jobs, including waitressing in a tea room, working at Yosemite and in a citrus packing house.

After graduating from Bible school both young women decided to go to Alaska as missionaries. In 1946 they traveled by train to Seattle where they boarded an Alaska steamship that took them to Seward. While onboard the vessel they held children's Bible classes. From Seward the twins traveled by small plane to Ninilchik where they helped Pauline Smith with her work. Eventually Marian married a local man, Nick Leman. Margaret's work in Ninilchik was cut short by a fall on ice that broke her leg. She was flown to Anchorage where she had surgery to insert a pin. The leg took a long time to heal so she stayed in Anchorage and began working as Johnny Gillespie's secretary at the Church of the Open Door, which is where I met her. During the summers she also helped out at Victory Bible Camp, a ministry that Johnny had started.

Those were busy days for both of us. Margaret was teaching a Sunday school girl's class, Child Evangelism classes and was Johnny's secretary. I was here and there helping where I could, but we found time to share our thoughts and our lives. In time we decided we should go see

56

Johnny concerning our relationship, so one evening we drove to Johnny and Nadine's home to seek their counsel. The result of that meeting was that we made plans for our wedding.

Things were happening so fast in my life I could hardly keep up with all the events of the past few months—salvation, new friends, different jobs, and now an approaching wedding day! It was all exciting, challenging and even frightening at times. Thinking of the responsibility of being married weighed heavily on my mind. Margaret was so kind and assured me she would be right with me all the way. This of course was another turning point in my life and Margaret's also. It was second only to believing on the Lord Jesus Christ for salvation—choosing a life mate is a most serious decision. With the wedding date set we started making plans for that day and the days afterwards.

The following Sunday Johnny announced our engagement by means of a Western Union Telegraph message, which stated that there was to be a temporary vacancy in the church office due to the wedding of Margaret Broady and Dave Lee on November 20, 1953. When this was read there was real excitement with much hand clapping, shouting, whistling and words of encouragement.

Our church family was so kind and helpful to us at this time. They showered us with gifts, arranged a reception, and decorated the church for the occasion. Due to the distance and expense neither Margaret's family nor mine were able to be with us for the wedding. Margaret's twin sister and family from Ninilchik were with us. Marian was Margaret's bridesmaid. My best man was our good friend Maver Roth. Our long-time friend Dan (Pop) Parmenter gave Margaret away. I still have a tape recording of the wedding ceremony with Johnny officiating. Our good friend and fellow missionary, John Hurt sang for us. It was a happy time for all.

The day after our wedding we climbed in my second-hand truck for a week at Victory Bible Camp, about 95 miles northeast of Anchorage. We could still drive in there, as the snow was not too deep. The week was spent cutting wood to keep warm in Floyd Gilman's un-insulated cabin. I remember stuffing old newspapers, rags and anything else in the cracks of the walls to keep the heat in and the cold out. We did some walking around the area.

In October I had filed an application for homesteading 150 acres from the VBC boundary down the valley to the Glenn Highway. Johnny had mentioned to me one day that this land was open for a homestead under the old homestead law. This really appealed to me as I wanted out of Anchorage for most any reason. I am not a city person.

Margaret was all for this idea also, as we wanted to work at VBC. With this in mind we looked the land over for our future cabin site. Several locations had their appeal, but we always came back to a spot just above the road and near the stream where we could get water. This location had access to the road and we could get water at very little cost. This was very important as neither of us had much money. I had been out of work for some time and Margaret didn't receive much income. We often joked that we married each other for our money! The Lord gave us a wonderful week there at VBC. In spite of the cold November temperatures, it was fun.

We enjoyed the isolation away from the highway and other signs of civilization. It was so quiet and peaceful in this true wilderness setting. An occasional moose would come by and there were lots of rabbits and winter birds to observe. What a great time we had and God gave us spiritual blessings also. It was just the two of us in His presence out there in His beautiful creation, getting to know each other better, reading the Word, praying and praising the Lord for His wonderful, loving kindness to His own.

Margaret preparing to fly to Ninilchik, 1946.

David and Margaret, November 20, 1953, at the Church of the Open Door.

Tanana

After the week at Victory Bible Camp, we drove back to Anchorage to begin a new assignment. Before we were married our good friends, Allen and Doris Franz, had asked if we would take their place in Tanana on the Yukon River, while they were "outside" (the Alaskan name for the lower 48 states). We traveled to Nenana by train, where Allen met us with his airplane and flew us to Tanana. This was a new place and experience for both of us, but we were happy to be there to serve the Lord and help the Franz's. Margaret, being the missionary that she was, went out to meet the people. She soon rounded up a few kids for a Bible class. I remember the little kids coming into the house all bundled up in fur coats so that all we could see were little round faces looking out.

Allen had a small Caterpillar tractor on tracks that he said I could use to haul firewood for the Northern Commercial Company. This gave me something to do, plus make a few dollars. The NC Company store was heated with a huge wood stove that took pieces of wood four feet long. They also sold the wood, so it gave me plenty of wood to haul. The firewood was already cut, so all I had to do was drive out to the woods and load it onto the sled. This went well until the temperature dropped close to 40 degrees below zero. There was not much daylight in December and January. I would start out as soon as I could dimly see the trail and try to make two trips each day. During the last load I would go home in the dark.

I remember one day I came to town as two dog teams met head on by the NC Company store. What a sight to see howling, fighting and growling dogs in mortal combat. The two Native mushers started beating the dogs to get them apart. I ran over and helped pull one sled back as the dogs were separated. To my amazement after they were untangled they were all able to walk and go on their way.

Tanana was divided in two parts, the white people on one end and the Native people in the other part. We lived in the Native end of town. All of this was very interesting to both of us as we observed the Native lifestyle. Most were very friendly and kind to us. One couple, Mr. Earhart and his Native wife Nettie, lived a short distance from town. Both were friendly and helpful. I asked Nettie if she would make me a pair of mittens like the Native men wore. This she did and they were so nice that I never wore them to work.

Mr. Earhart told me he came from Montana over land, up through Canada. He started out with horses and ended up with a dog team. It took two years to make the journey. While in the Tanana area he made his living cutting and hauling firewood for the steam boats operating on the Yukon River. The wood business was all done during the winter months. Mr. Earhart was one of those old time Alaskans who never left the state.

After some weeks of extreme cold, around negative 50 degrees, it warmed up to zero. I remember it felt like a spring day. In March, Allen and Doris came back and we returned to Anchorage. How good the Lord was to give us this time in Tanana. More could be said about how we lived out there, such as getting our water through a hole cut in the ice on the Yukon River, the people we met and the Native lifestyle before snowmachines. We shared our life together in an unfamiliar setting. I remember how Margaret craved peaches after we realized she was pregnant. There were no peaches in the store so I ordered some canned peaches by air on the next plane from Fairbanks.

While in the Anchorage area we stayed with our close friends Maver and Carmen Roth until it was time to start out to our homestead. To realize maximum Veterans credit we had to be on the land within five months from the time of entry. That meant we had to be there by March 1954, because entry was filed October 30th 1953, at the land office in Anchorage. We bought supplies and made preparation for the next phase of our lives.

The Homestead

I don't remember the exact date we left for the homestead, only that it was sometime in March, 1954. One bright day, with a great deal of excitement, we loaded the Chevy pickup with our supplies for the trip up the Glenn Highway to the homestead. We weren't youngsters anymore, being in our thirties, but we were a happy couple looking forward to the coming months on our homestead.

We left Maver and Carmen's home and headed up the scenic Glenn Highway—past Fort Richardson, Eagle River, the historic Eklutna Native settlement and the Eklutna flats (where during the summer masses of wild Iris bloom). As we drove toward Palmer, we saw the Chugach Mountains to the south, with Pioneer peak overlooking the Knik River.

Palmer was a small town with fertile farm land all around. The Matanuska Valley was settled during the 1930's with the Federal Government assisting settlers from the northern states to clear and farm the land. This was all so interesting for me, coming from a farm myself. It was very attractive land with good soil and moderate temperatures.

We drove through Palmer then Sutton, a coal mining town. The Glenn Highway was built on the railroad bed that once went to the Chickaloon coal fields. Next to the road, a good part of the way, was the Matanuska River. The high, rugged Chugach Mountain Range was on the south side of the river and the Talkeetna Mountains on the north. After crossing the Chickaloon River, the road starts climbing, with the river far below. At about mile 90 we could see the massive expanse of the Matanuska Glacier in the distance. From this point the highway descended to where we turned off onto what would later be named Victory Road.

Arriving at Mile 95 on this bright, sunshiny March day, I realized it would be impossible to drive up the road, as the snow was much too deep. However, we were prepared for this. We had a military double-ended sled for hauling in our supplies and we each had snowshoes. Mine were regular trail shoes and Margaret's were the smaller bear paw snowshoes. We unloaded all of our supplies at the end of the road before I drove the truck back a couple miles to the highway maintenance camp where I left it for safe keeping.

I walked back to where Margaret was waiting to snowshoe in. I walked first to make a better trail for bringing the stuff in. Margaret did very well with the bear paw snow shoes as long as she stayed on the trail. I pulled the loaded sled while Margaret hiked along behind. I tried to make it as easy as possible for her because she was pregnant and her right leg was still weaker than the other leg because of being broken several years before.

Getting our stuff in was work, but it was fun. We were on our own land! On one trip with the loaded sled we came to where the trail went downhill for some distance. Since by that time we had a packed trail, I decided to send the sled down by itself, expecting it to stay on the trail. However, there was a turn about halfway down where the sled jumped the trail and hit a stump. Everything went flying into the snow bank. Not much was lost, except some of the eggs. This was all part of the adventure of getting our supplies in.

One of the first things we did was set up a tent on the location where we planned to build our future home. It was too cold to stay in the tent, so we moved into a cabin that our friends, the Gilman's owned, on camp property. After getting somewhat settled in, I set to work clearing trees from the site where we were to build our little cabin. Since the snow was about two feet deep when I cut down the trees, later after it melted I had to go around and cut the stumps level to the ground. Everyday life under those conditions takes a lot of time—clearing land, cutting firewood, hauling water, making meals, and washing clothes under rigorous conditions. This was not really new for me as it was the way I grew up. Margaret did a wonderful job with her part of the work.

At this point I would like to say that while I enjoyed the trip to the homestead, I was not alone in this. Margaret was right there by my side and we were in this project together. It was wonderful to have a wife to talk with about everything. Margaret loved the outdoors, the flowers, berry picking, mushroom hunting, birds and gardening. She would see pictures in the clouds and ask, "Don't you see?" whatever she was looking at. Often times I just didn't see what she saw.

Margaret was steadfast in her faith and never doubted, that I know of. At this time I still struggled with the assurance of my salvation, though without a doubt I knew God had spoken to me in a most vivid and powerful way that I would never forget. I believe the Holy Spirit revealed to me the terrifying painful, dreadful blackness of hell forever. At that time my mind and heart were turned to the God of Light. It was truly a brilliant white, pure light. In I John the Scriptures tell us that God is a God of Light.

It was a great experience to be here on our homestead in the quietness of the wilderness setting. There is a feeling that is hard to express in words when you are in the true wilderness, out of sight and sound of civilization. So there we were, just the two of us, and happy as could be. It seemed like we had the whole country to roam around in. I would snowshoe for miles around just for the fun of it. Margaret did not travel far until her leg grew stronger.

In the spring the bears came out of hibernation and we would see them occasionally. There were white Dall sheep on the mountains above us and moose in the area as well. Sometimes caribou would come down to the lake. There was much to see and do.

When the snow melted enough to drive up the trail we had a little more freedom. Taking the pickup truck, I drove down to Palmer to a sawmill for material to build our cabin. I considered building with logs, but had no chain saw and very little equipment. The quickest and most economical way for us was to buy the lumber for the cabin. I had the foundation, the floor joists and the floor done when Maver and Carmen came to lend a hand. Maver was a very skilled carpenter so his help was much appreciated. With the two of us working we soon had the little two room cabin built and ready to move in.

During the summer months we both worked at Victory Bible Camp, helping out where needed. At the end of the summer camping season I took down the tents and closed the camp for the winter. It was a good summer for us.

The fall of 1954 was a real good blueberry year. I could pick a five gallon container in a very short time. If anyone came by we would share the blueberries. It was also a good year for rabbits. They were running everywhere. One day I shot a black bear right below our cabin, which I dressed out for meat. Another time a wolverine came loping by and once a lynx strolled past on his big padded feet. It was a good time for us, with lovely weather. We could pick berries, hike up the mountain to see the sheep and hunt, mostly for small game. The fall colors were beautiful.

As summer ended and fall came on we had to decide what to do for the winter. When September came it was getting cooler, the first light snow fell and the laundry was freezing on the line. We drove to the small town of Glennallen to wait for Margaret to deliver the baby. Our Doctor was James Pinneo at Faith Hospital, a mission hospital. Finally the time came and we had a baby boy on September 4. We named him Brian Charles Lee. Everything went well and we were soon back at the homestead cabin. This was a blessing and a challenge at the same time. Brian was healthy and Margaret was great with the little fellow, but we both realized we could not stay there for the winter in an un-insulated cabin. Plus we were broke by then.

David, Margaret and Brian at their Indiana home.

Evidence of a successful sheep hunt, 1960.

Trip To California & Indiana, 1954-1956

The decision was made to go "Outside" to see our parents as it had been several years since we had seen them (three for me, eight for Margaret). The next question was how to finance the trip. The only asset we had was land and a pickup truck. I spoke to Pop Parmenter about our need to go Outside. The solution was for us to sell forty acres, the cabin and the pickup truck to Pop for $900. This was not much, but enough to get us started.

With the money in hand, we bought two plane tickets to Seattle, WA. When we arrived in Seattle we had to stay all night in the airport. At that time Alaska was still a Territory so when we came to the lower forty-eight states we had to go through customs as if we were entering from a foreign country. By the time we got to the custom station it was closed for the night. We could go no further until we cleared customs. So there we were with a new little baby, waiting out the night. As I remember we had bottles and milk, but didn't know how to heat the milk. Margaret thought of a solution by heating the bottle under the hot running water in the rest room. Praise the Lord He was with us and we all survived the night though it seemed like a very long one.

After clearing customs we went by Greyhound bus to California to see Margaret's parents. I remember the trip on the bus so well because whenever the bus stopped Brian would start to cry, but when we started moving again the crying stopped. The other passengers took note of this also though no one complained. We arrived safely in San Dimas to be with Margaret's parents for a few days. It was good for me to meet them and they were very kind to me.

At that time the San Dimas area was growing lots of oranges and lemons. I could see why the Broady's moved from Nebraska to

California. It was a very pleasant place with a wonderful climate and citrus groves. We met Margaret's friends and church family. Over the years I have regretted that I was not in a position to get to know my father-in-law better. Frank had a good education with a degree in agriculture. He was very active in civic affairs in the community.

From the homestead to Southern California was a change, though not a shock. Our times are in God's hands and we both felt it was His will for us to be in San Dimas with family and friends for awhile. After staying for about two weeks we felt it was time for us to move on to Indiana to meet my parents. This also was to be another change and milestone in our earthly and spiritual journey.

Psalm 107:8-9 says "Oh that men would praise the Lord for His loving kindness and for His wonderful works to the children of men. For He satisfies the longing soul and fills the hungry with goodness." When I left the farm and home three and a half years earlier I was a defeated, desperate, spiritually dead person with no hope. But God in His mercy and grace saw fit to claim me for His own.

I left home with one small suitcase and now I was returning with a godly wife and little son. Even above that blessing I was now and forever a born again believer in Christ Jesus my Savior. I now had a reason to live and a sure hope for the future. I had many things to learn from the Lord on our journey. In my heart I longed to know this God of light and loving kindness better.

When I left home in May, 1951, I just up and left everything—my equipment, livestock, everything. Thankfully my father took care of it for me. Margaret and I talked things over and decided to stay on the farm for a while. The house on grandfather Lee's farm was empty so we moved in with little furniture. We started a farming business with chickens and hogs. It takes time to get even a small operation going to bring in some income. I was happy to be back on the farm again and had some plans in mind for the future.

With not much income coming in I got a job at a plant in Bedford cutting building blocks of limestone with a diamond saw. In the spring of 1955 I planted the crops with the help of my father and a neighbor. At that time we needed a refrigerator and with the hot weather coming on it was essential that we get one. We bought a new refrigerator from a store in Bedford on time payments. My, how hard it was to make payments when there was very little money. We decided then and there that when we got it paid for we would never again buy on time payment.

Again, Margaret, the missionary, rounded up some neighbor kids for a game night and short Bible lesson. This was a good group of teenage kids. It went very well and the kids seemed to enjoy their time in our humble house. I know in later years that more than one of the kids told us how they enjoyed the meetings. To be honest I never felt it was my gift to be the leader in a youth ministry. However, with all of my hesitation and lack of leadership, if the Lord used our efforts to His glory, the praise goes to Him.

In the early spring I made maple syrup again since I still had the equipment. I always enjoyed tapping the maple trees, gathering the sap and boiling it down to syrup. I felt I was making some progress on the farm. The chickens were producing very well with several cases of eggs to sell each week. A neighbor picked up our eggs to sell and our hogs were ready to go to market in Cincinnati.

We were going to a small church in a little town two miles down the road. Margaret helped with their Bible School that summer. Neither one of us were very happy at that church because there didn't seem to be much spiritual life. During this time I took short correspondence courses from Moody Bible Institute and one from Back to the Bible. I also worked through a Navigator's Bible Memory Course.

Another blessing came January 16, 1956 when our second son, Daniel Max, was born on a cold, blustery winter day in the hospital in Seymour, Indiana. I think Dan holds it against us to this day that he was not born in Alaska. Anyway, I got mother and son home safely in spite of the weather.

One day Margaret came to me in tears saying that she just hated this place on the farm, and the house in particular. I know the house is a woman's domain and she should be happy there. This was a shock to me, though I knew she had trouble understanding the people. Life on a farm was so new to her and the people talked differently. Margaret would say to me, "What did they say?" and I had to interpret the local lingo. However, I knew she was well liked by one and all. This was a very sad time for both of us.

Margaret was never one to complain. She faced difficulties with courage, strength and faith in God. So when Margaret came to me in such a state of sadness I realized we were facing a crisis, or what could be one. The concern as I saw it was that we were going in two different directions. I had explained to Margaret before we were married that I had a farm in Indiana. I felt a strong desire to be back on the farm, while Margaret was called to Alaska to be a missionary and I am sure she still had this in mind. We discussed all this at some length.

I was torn between two desires, or I guess I could say three. One was to go wherever God would lead us. The second was to comfort my faithful wife in her unhappiness. And the third was how I would deal with the matter of the farm. I remembered shortly after the Lord called me to Himself that I talked to Johnny about what I should do, now that I was a born again believer. Should I go back to the farm or pursue some other occupation. Johnny's response was an emphatic "No, do not to go back to the farm." I also talked to Marv Webber, Floyd Gilman and Pop Parmenter, three men I highly respected as mature men of the faith. All three were of the same opinion that the farm was out and it was not the thing for me to do.

Then I read Luke 14:2-6 about hating father, mother, wife, children and brethren. I concluded, wrongly, at that time that anything I desired to do was sin, including being a farmer. I so earnestly, with all my heart, wanted the mind of the Lord as to which direction I should go, that I was willing to give it up if that was the Lord's will. I know Margaret and I both wanted to follow the Lord in all matters.

When Margaret came to me with such sadness of heart, the question of discerning the Lord's will came into focus once again. All things considered, it seemed that the right thing to do was to prepare to go back to Alaska. It wasn't that I didn't like Alaska; it is a great state and I was thankful to have experienced life on the Last Frontier. Plus, we had made so many wonderful friends in ministry and working on jobs there.

As my dear wife revealed her feelings to me I realized we faced a major decision. What was the Lord telling me to do in this situation?

While I would have been happy to remain on the farm doing what I liked to do, I felt the real necessity was to meet the needs of my wife. One thing we had in our favor was that if we had any differences we could talk and pray to God about the matter. Shortly after this talk we made the decision to sell out and go back to Alaska.

I was not thrilled about this decision, but if that was what the Lord was telling us to do, then regardless of my feelings I was willing to go. I know we both felt the need to work through this difference with the Lord's help. The thought of separation or divorce never entered either of our minds. When we were married we promised to stay together until death took us home and we meant it with all of our hearts.

Having made this decision to go back to Alaska, I contacted an auctioneer to have a farm sale. Advertisements were prepared and placed around the country. I gathered together all of our equipment and stuff that we wanted to sell at the auction. I asked a good neighbor, Asher Baker, to be the clerk for the sale and he was glad to do that for us. By this time my equipment was well worn so we didn't realize very much money from the sale.

With that taken care of, we needed to decide how we were to get back to Alaska. One day I read in a farm paper about a farmer who built a home-made camper for the bed of his pickup. This looked like something that I could do. First I used some of the money from the farm sale to buy a good used pickup to put the camper on, a 1954 3/4 ton. Then I went to town and bought the materials needed to build the camper. We soon had the camper ready for the trip with the help of a neighbor, Everet McKeaigg, including an apartment size gas cook stove and a bed across the front end. With the house closed up and supplies in place we said goodbye to my parents and departed in April, 1956.

Back To Alaska

Leaving my parents at the farm, we drove to Medora, Indiana to get some money from the account we had there. Now came another shock—there was no money left in our account. Somehow I had not kept good records on the money spent. We were confronted with a real dilemma. The house we just left was empty and we had said good-by to parents and neighbors. In effect we had burned our bridges behind us. The only money we had was what we each had in our pocket book and purse, which was not very much. After counting the money at hand, we decided we had enough to buy gas for the trip to see Margaret's parents in California.

So off we went, starting a 9,600 mile journey to Alaska with two little boys and very little money. I'm not sure if that was faith or presumption. Dan was just a few weeks old at the time. The trip to California went well. The next decision we had to face was how to continue on our journey to Alaska without enough money. Visiting with Margaret's parents and puttering with the camper, we put in time in California. Almost two weeks went by when I received a letter from my father. In this letter was a check. Dad and I had bought a chainsaw together and this was my half of the chainsaw. With this check and what little money we had left we decided to drive on to Alaska. We didn't tell either of our parents that we were short of cash. Very likely they would have helped us on our way. Margaret's parents were very kind to us and I'm glad we had this time with them.

We also spent time with Margaret's sister, Betty, and her two children. It was enjoyable to be where Margaret grew up. It was a pleasant place with orange and lemon groves, small farms and fruit trees in the back yard of their home. California was a very fruitful state. Leaving that good land and the family, we traveled up through California. Just saying we drove up through California doesn't do justice to the state. The distance we traveled included towns, country, big trees and National Parks. It is truly a spectacular and magnificent state.

The next state, Oregon, had its own beauty. We stopped to visit my cousins near Cottage Grove. Bob and Lenore lived on a small farm not far out of town. It was a real nice place to live and it was enjoyable to see them again. From Bob and Lenore's farm we trucked north through Seattle and Bellingham and then crossed into Canada at Sumas. The truck was running well and the camper met our needs. The little boys traveled well.

Dan slept in his basket at night on top of the cook stove. Brian had a nice little nest under our bed, while the two of us had the big bed. Margaret kept busy taking care of Brian and Dan; she was so loving and careful with the boys. We were having a good time and enjoyed the trip. I have always liked trips we have made over the years. There is something about seeing the different areas of the United States and Canada. Every area has its attraction and points of interest. As always, I know the Lord was with us every mile of the way.

We traveled through the Canadian Rockies, connecting with the Alaska Highway at Dawson Creek. It was slow going from there on, with spring break-up and the gravel road which was very soft much of the way. Our truck had sixteen inch wheels so we could get through the mud-holes where cars would get stuck. Several times we had to stop while road repairs were made. At one point there was a mud slide which blocked the road. I had a good shovel and axe so with the help of two other stranded men we soon had a narrow path around the point.

We usually stopped for the night at any suitable gravel pit to get some rest. We just didn't have enough money to get a motel room. Besides, we had a good bed in the homemade camper and food to eat. The only thing we bought was gasoline for the truck. There were frequent stops for gas as we didn't get very good gas mileage. I remember the time we stopped at Coal River for gas and it was 71 cents per gallon. This ate into our funds pretty heavily.

So on we drove through the vast wilderness of British Columbia and the Yukon Territory, all parts of God's wonderful creation—what a great God we serve! (Psalm 145:2-3) It was slow going all the way because of the soft road and mud holes. We did well to make 300 miles each day and sometimes not even that many miles. In time we arrived at the Alaskan border and were in the U.S. again. I remember how good it felt to be driving on blacktop road. We drove on to Anchorage to regroup and plan for the near future. The Lord was certainly with us all the way. How thankful we were for his strength and protection.

Anchorage (1956-1957)

Since we were practically broke, I had to seek employment. I soon found a job with the Anchorage School District as a janitor. This was not exactly my cup of tea, but I felt the job was needed for the short term. One problem was that they only paid us once a month so we had to wait for a whole month to get the first paycheck. By then we were flat broke. Using our last few nickels Margaret bought some milk for Dan. The rest of us did without. I know if we had asked for help any number of friends would have helped us through this period. Anyway, with the Lord's help we survived.

I worked the night shift through the summer and the following winter. When spring came I got off so we could go back to VBC for the summer. The job met our needs at that time. That first winter we lived in a little house on 9th and L Street in Anchorage. Actually the house was a shack and when we moved out the city condemned it and it was destroyed. The next winter we were in a house that belonged to a friend who served at VBC.

While in Anchorage we were able to attend the Church of the Open Door where we had started from several years earlier. It was good to be back there. The church was growing, so there was a need for more space. The decision was made to buy property for a new church building. When this was done and the little log church on Fourth Avenue was sold two things happened: a new church was built and, sadly, there was a church split.

I realized we were on a spiritual journey with all its joys, sorrows, trials and testing, as well as a physical journey. We are strangers and pilgrims here on earth. But praise God we are not alone. He is a God of loving kindness and He cares for His own. I remind myself often that I am "In Christ". Galatians 2:20—For I am crucified with Christ never the less I live, yet not I but Christ lives in me and the life which I now live in the flesh I live by the faith of the Son of God who loved me and gave himself for me. We were one in Christ and still together, in good health and Brian and Dan were thriving, all thanks to our heavenly Father.

In the fall of 1957 we returned to Anchorage, where I resumed my job with the Anchorage School District. That time we stayed in the home of a friend, Pearl Wright, whom we knew from church and camp.

Dan & Pearl Parmenter

Isn't God good to give us friends to help us on our journey of life? I met Mom and Pop Parmenter the first summer I was in Alaska. As a new believer I wanted to be around my new Christian friends as much as possible. I would go to the little log church on Fourth Ave. in Anchorage and talk with Pastor John Gillespie. Johnny was so helpful, answering my questions and giving me advice.

One day I was at the church when Pop Parmenter came in. Johnny said I should get acquainted with Pop. I soon got to know Pop and found this man to be a very interesting fellow. He had so many stories to tell about his growing up days in Nebraska, World War I in the Navy, living in Wyoming with his wife, coming to Alaska in 1935, working on the railroad and then being employed at Anchorage International Airport in airport security. Pop had stories to tell about everything he was involved in.

We heard his stories so many times over the years and yet I cannot remember them well enough to repeat. The stories were always the same, never varied and always word for word at each telling. One time Margaret and I were at their house for a visit. As we were about to leave Pop started to tell one of his stories. Mom Parmenter said to us, "This is a long one so you might as well sit down." Mom was always so patient as he told his stories. Mom did object when Pop would come to our house and start talking while Margaret was teaching Brian and Dan. Margaret was homeschooling the boys when we were living in the trapper's cabin.

After we came back to Alaska in the spring of 1956, we stayed in the cabin we had sold since Mom and Pop were not using it at the time. Later when Pop retired from the airport security job he and Mom came to live in the cabin. Pop dug a half basement under the cabin and added a nice size living room to the upstairs. I helped him and his son, Danny, dig the dirt out for the basement. This made the house a very comfortable home for the two of them.

Over the years I had many hunting trips with Pop. One day he came over and asked if I would like to drive up the highway to hunt for caribou. Driving along, we spotted a small band of caribou close to the highway. Pop stopped immediately and we jumped out and started shooting. When the shooting stopped, we counted and discovered we had shot more than we were permitted, which was a problem! Just at the right time John Van Wingerden came by on his way home from Glennallen. Seeing us cutting up the animals, he offered to take the excess caribou that we had killed. I'm sure I shot two with one shot because when I went over to check on the one there were two lying side by side.

In 1976 Pop's health declined to the point they needed help. The decision was made to move to the Pioneer Home in Palmer. Before they made the move we talked about the house and decided to buy it back. I asked Pop what he wanted for the property. The price was $6,000, so I wrote a check, then we rented the house to InterAct Mission until 1980 when we sold the Parmenter's house to them.

Victory Bible Camp (1958)

While working at camp the summer of 1958 we stayed in our homestead cabin. Mom and Pop Parmenter were not using it at that time. In fact it was as we had left it, with even a Farm Journal magazine I had left there in 1954. Of course this made me think of the farm we had left.

After working at VBC that summer, Johnny asked if we would like to stay all winter at the camp. The camp had more equipment and property to look after and plans were being made for some winter camps. This was exciting, as our desire was to work at the camp. In preparations for the winter so we insulated a building at camp, at the time called the Craft House, where we would live.

We were very comfortable, with a wood burning barrel stove for heat. Before it got too cold and snowy, I cut a good supply of fire wood. We hauled all our water up from the spring-fed stream by our homestead cabin. Of course this activity took much of our time. It was so wonderful to be out of Anchorage and at camp. We were there by ourselves, with two little boys to entertain us.

I shot a moose right at the end of Index Lake so all I had to do was row across the lake, load the meat in the boat, and head back to the dock where I could drive down with the pickup. I also went sheep hunting with Gale VanDiest up on Anthracite Ridge. That was my first sheep and we discovered that sheep meat is really good eating.

One winter day I was bird hunting around Index Lake when I saw a game trail out on the frozen lake. Going out to investigate, I discovered to my surprise that the tracks were made by caribou rather than moose. My curiosity aroused, I took off after them. I could easily track them because there was 8-10 inches of snow on the ground. I was carrying two guns, a 22 rifle for spruce hens or ptarmigan and a model 70 Winchester 300 HH rifle. I was in good condition with all the walking I had been doing. With some effort I finally caught up to a small herd of caribou. The problem was by that time they were high up on the mountain and just starting to cross the boulder field at the foot of Victory Peak. I hesitated briefly wondering if I should shoot in the boulder area.

I picked out one caribou and fired, but he fell out of sight. Thinking I had missed, I shot at another one and he did the same thing. Before the herd moved out of sight I fired once more and saw where that one fell. After field dressing the caribou, I thought I should check on where I had shot at the other two and discovered I had killed those two also! Now I had my hands full because the first two had fallen down out of sight between the huge boulders. First I had to tie a rope on their antlers and haul them up to where I could work on dressing them out. This was all enjoyable, though plenty of work. I worked all day and it took me two more days to drag them down to our cabin. This gave us a full supply of good meat. We ate a lot of meat those days.

With winter and more snow coming on I made a snow plow. It was a crude affair made out of heavy timber with a grader blade spiked to the bottom edge as a cutting edge. I attached it to the front of the camp's ton-and-a-half truck. With a heavy load on the truck and dual chains on the wheels I could move some snow.

Occasionally the highway camp foreman at mile 90 on the Glenn highway would drive in to visit and check on us. I enjoyed his visits. He was older than we were and had years of experience in Alaska. Another neighbor we made friends with was a young man by the name of Martin Vorheis. He lived in a trapper's cabin on the other side of the Matanuska River. Martin was quite an interesting fellow. He was a graduate of Yale University and aspired to be a writer like Ernest Hemingway. Martin made a living trapping, guiding and writing. He was a big man, 6 feet 4 inches and in good physical condition because of his guiding and trapping. I would snowshoe over to see him from time to time. Though Martin was not a Christian we got along very well. For transportation he had an old jeep truck he left at our place. We would take the battery into our house to keep it warm and then help him start his jeep.

VICTORY BIBLE CAMP (1958)

Another neighbor we got to know quite well was Mr. Williams who was a professional trapper. At this time he was trapping the white Dall sheep for a zoo. His camp was a double wide tent high up Muddy Creek. He was a very friendly man with years of experience in Alaska. When He caught a sheep he would get Martin to help pack the animal down to the road.

Laundry was a two day affair. We had to get enough water and heat it, then use the scrub board. Hanging the laundry on a line in the house caused lots of moisture. On a cold day when the door was opened it would cause steam to billow up and we could hardly see for a few minutes. Some things we hung outdoors on a line to freeze dry. There was no electricity for lights or appliances. We used Coleman lanterns and Aladdin lamps for light and a gas iron for ironing.

We had a good battery radio for news and other programs. On Sunday we could hear Charles Fuller with The Old Fashioned Revival Hour and Radio Bible Class for the evening sermon. M. R. DeHaan was a wonderful teacher. Margaret was very careful to dress up the boys for Sunday. She would give them a flannel graph Bible lesson. We used a caribou hide for a rug near our bed that was so warm and soft. Brian at this time was starting to talk some and he called the caribou rug the "prayer uggin" He couldn't pronounce his "r's" yet. The only problem with the prayer rug was that it shed hair all over the place.

Margaret's home church in San Dimas had given her money to help in her missionary work and continued to support us since we were working at Victory Bible Camp. Then the White River Baptist Church in Indiana started to help us with $50.00 a month. Two of our dear friends here in Alaska helped us with a monthly check also. Since Margaret was a charter member of Alaska Mission the mission allowed some of our income to come through their books. This was a real encouragement to us and kept us in contact with our supporting churches.

I felt we had a successful winter at VBC. When spring came it was time to prepare for the coming camping season. The equipment, power plant, water system and plumbing needed to be checked out. Marvin Webber was a plumber and did much of the work at the camp.

Victory High School (1959)

The year of 1959 was a year that brought some changes that would affect our lives for many years to come. Victory High School started in the fall of that year, on land adjacent to VBC. Wally and Alice Bays, with their new baby, came to be the principal and first teachers. This took a lot of planning on the part of Wally and Alice. Wally helped at camp for much of the summer, plus prepared to get the high school program started. I have such a high regard for Wally and Alice Bays because of their dedication to the task and the great effort they put into this project.

One of the first things that needed to be done was build a house for them and the first students to live in. Lumber was ordered and I went into Anchorage with the camp truck to haul it out to the site. I remember backing the truck on the trail near where the building was to be built. During the missionary conference that summer the men gathered around and got the house framed and the roof on. Then all the men left for their ministries around the state. That left Wally and me, and Wally had more than he could handle already. Alice's 70 year old father came up to help. Fortunately he was a good carpenter which I was not. We got the house ready, but it was some time before they had a heating stove. I enjoyed working with Mr. Johnson, Alice's godly father.

One other project was to build an outhouse. With no lumber at hand and no money for such, I went to the woods with a chain saw and came back with logs to build it. As Wally said, it was Alaska's stoutest log outhouse. They were ready when the first students arrived. Wally used a trapper's cabin for a classroom that first winter.

Another wonderful blessing came to us on July 23rd when Margaret delivered our precious little daughter, Sharon Ruth, at the hospital in

Glennallen. This was truly an exciting year for all of us. That same year Alaska became the 49th state and we have never been the same since. Also VBC was starting winter camps. This was quite a challenge to get the buildings heated, trails shoveled and water hauled for the kitchen.

I well remember one camp during the spring break in March. It was 35 degrees below zero, but we managed very well. The kids really enjoyed their experience, especially sledding down the hill onto Index Lake. There were many spills when they didn't make the turns on the way down. I rode quite a few times myself. I hung Coleman lanterns in the trees to give light along the sledding trail to the lake. When the campers got too cold they went inside for games and food. It was a fun time in spite of the cold. It was good to see VBC being used year around. Truly the Lord was doing a work here in this little valley, with increased attendance for the summer camps and now the winter camps.

When the summer camps were over Johnny liked to go hunting. Many times he asked me to go with him and his boys. I came to think I was almost part of the family. That fall we each got a nice Dall sheep. We were in a very good position here for sheep hunting as we could hike up the mountain right above our house, then go through the pass onto Anthracite Ridge. The view from the mountain was spectacular. From some points we could look down on the camp area, Index Lake and Shallow Lake, then onto the Matanuska River and the great white mass of the Matanuska Glacier.

What a creation our God has put here for our use and enjoyment. Psalm 104 speaks of God's creation and verse 18 speaks of the high hills as a refuge for the wild goats and the rocks for badgers. Psalm 104:24 "How many are your works, O Lord, in wisdom you made them all; the earth is full of your creatures."

Indiana (1960 – 1962)

The journey continued with another decision to go "Outside" to see our parents. It had been about three years since we last saw them and now we had Sharon to show them. With the distance and expense involved we just couldn't afford to make the trip very often. Retracing the route of our previous trip, we made it to the farm. The only incident was that we blew a tire about 50 miles above Fort Nelson. I remember when we stopped to check the flat tire Brian and Dan thought it was so funny for some reason. I didn't think it was funny. I had an old tire for a spare and I put that on until we could get to Fort Nelson where we bought a new tire for $70.00. That of course made a dent in our meager funds. The Lord was so good in allowing us safe passage on another long journey. Praise the Lord.

The next question we faced was what to do next. As I checked the options it seemed like a few dairy cows would give a quicker return for the money. I didn't make any of these decisions without talking it over with Margaret—for better or worse we were in this together. She was willing to try the old house once again, so I went to the bank in Medora to make arrangements for funds to buy a few dairy cows.

With the banks approval I found a local farmer who had the right cattle. I located some good looking cows in a nearby county which I was able to purchase. Getting set up for milking and getting the cows home was quite a task. In a short time we were set up and had milk to sell each day. One good cow was injured while loading them at the farm of the seller. Finally we had to send her to market. This project was working very well for us and the cows were paying for themselves with the bank loan. The spring of 1961 I planted crops, put up hay and later that fall we filled the silo with corn silage for cow feed. This was to be the last time the silo was ever filled.

This year was an eventful one for us with the farm work. We sent Brian to the local grade school for his first grade and we started attending a small Baptist church about eight miles away. This was to be our church home when we were in Indiana. They later took on supporting us at VBC.

I was making progress on the farm, but I sensed Margaret was not as happy as we would like, so again we made the decision to go back to Alaska. I shipped the remaining cows off and sold out once again. At the same time I decided I would get this farming idea out of my mind once and for all, so I sold our little farm to a good neighbor who wanted to retire and live there. As it turned out this elderly couple lived there until they died. In April of 1962 we took Brian out of school early to go back to Alaska and VBC. After paying all the expenses we still had a few hundred dollars left from the sale of the farm.

Once again as we journeyed to Alaska, we went by way of California. Life is a spiritual journey also and we did seek to know the will of the Lord in these matters. It had always been my desire that whatever we did we would be together as a family and I know that was Margaret's desire also. So whether on the farm or at VBC we would be together. God certainly provided for us in the years to come. Romans 8:28 tells us, "And we know that in all things God works for the good of those who love him who have been called according to his purpose."

Back in Indiana as a family of five. Back row: Margaret, Sharon, David.
Front row: Dan, Brian.

Fishing in Ninilchik—Loren Leman and Dave pitching fish into a
cannery truck, while Wayne (in back) and Nick look on.

In front of the fishing cabin in Ninilchik. Dan and Dave in back,
Margaret, Sharon and Brian sitting.

Commercial Fishing

In the early sixties we started commercial fishing with Nick Leman. This gave us summer work for several years. I'm thankful that this gave us money to live on, but I didn't enjoy fishing. I found working for Nick to be the most difficult, stressful thing I had ever done in all my life. The hard work did not bother me as I was used to working hard. It was the continual shouting and yelling when we were fishing. This certainly stretched my patience to the limit at times. Also the coastal climate was depressing, with the damp, rainy weather and the low-hanging clouds overhead. I know I have many faults of my own, so I go to God in prayer confessing my many sins and seeking His forgiveness, as it says in I John 1:9. As believers of Christ Jesus we are to forgive others as Christ forgave us (Col. 3:13).

Each summer when the season was over we would pack up in a hurry and take off for home. Along the way we would stop in Soldotna for a quart of ice cream. This was special for all of us because we usually didn't have the money for this kind of treat. Another treat was when we would stop in Palmer to buy a chicken. After eating moose and caribou meat all winter this was a great change for us. Much more could be said about those fishing years. Margaret really enjoyed being with her twin sister and they had much to talk about. We liked our little fishing cabin on the beach, the delicious salmon that we would can, and the king salmon we brought home each year.

Homestead Life

After returning from Indiana, the camp let us stay in a little trapper's cabin, situated beside Shallow Lake. In their early school years, Margaret homeschooled Brian and Dan. Wally Bays loaned us two used school desks. Margaret took this school work very seriously and she did a good job.

During our time in the cabin we enjoyed good grayling fishing. It was no trouble to catch one or two 15 to 18 inch fish for breakfast. During the coldest part of the winter I would cut ice blocks to be stored in an old cabin on the property for use at camp. The ice would last all summer. Most likely, using ice cut from the lake would not go over these days with the Health Department, but in those days it worked for us and no one died from it that I know of.

One time as I was going to work at camp I spotted a black bear across the lake from the cabin. I rushed back to the cabin, grabbed my trusty 300 HH rifle and took careful aim. When the bear came running through a small clearing I fired and down he went. The Gillespie kids heard the shot and came over to see what the action was all about. Another time a bear tried to break down the door to the Trapper's cabin. My first thought was to shoot it through the door, but decided that wasn't a good idea. I waited until the bear walked around the cabin, then stepped out and shot it.

One time in the early years of Victory High School they were about out of meat, so Wally approached Pop Parmenter and me about going on a winter caribou hunt. At that time Pop and I were always ready for a hunting trip. The school had an Army 4x4 that we decided to use for hauling the meat. It wasn't licensed for road travel, so Pop hitched it to his truck and we towed it to Eureka Lodge. The only problem was that

Wally, who was steering the 4x4, often couldn't see because of flying snow. We parked the truck and drove the 4x4 several miles away from the highway, where we found a herd of caribou. We split up and began shooting, taking down six animals.

It was a cold day with about a foot of snow on the ground, but we were warm enough as we worked on field dressing the caribou. When we got the caribou loaded onto the 4x4 it wouldn't start. After working on it for quite a while we gave up and started walking out. It was getting colder, but we kept warm with the walking, and the moon was full so we had plenty of light. At the highway we talked to some men that told us the temperature was negative 42! Then we had to work on Pop's truck to get it started. He had a plumber's torch that he placed under the oil pan to warm it up. Soon we were on our way and arrived home safely, but without the meat we had set out to get.

When we went back we found everything just as we had left it. It took some time, but we were able to get the 4x4 started. On our way to the highway, we spun out on a steep hill. We decided to run a cable up to a tree and use the front-end winch. This worked well until the winch started jumping out of gear. Finally, I laid on the hood and reached out to hold the winch lever. We were making headway until all six caribou slid out the back of the truck. With some effort we got all six stiff, frozen caribou back into the 4x4 and struggled on up the hill. After that we had no more trouble. Praise the Lord for supplying the much needed meat for VHS staff and students, and for protecting us through the extreme cold.

Earthquake

The exciting event of 1964 was the March 27, Good Friday earthquake. That old trapper's cabin really shook and when it was over there was a six inch wide crack in the floor. I remember the cat coming up through the crack afterward. It was impossible to keep the cupboard doors closed during the quake, so we just got out of the way and let things fly. We lost a few dishes and the dinner Margaret was cooking on the wood stove. It was at this time that we had the dining hall at camp up on temporary posts in order to excavate and enlarge the basement area. I was afraid to look at the dining hall, fully expecting the whole building to have gone over the bank. Much to my surprise and delight there was very little damage to the building, only broken dishes in the kitchen. That brought much praise to the Lord for His protection.

We managed to stay in the trapper's cabin until the summer, and then we were offered a used house trailer. Pop Parmenter towed the trailer out from Anchorage to a house site near the homestead cabin. Our good friend, Ernie Lucia, offered us building materials from their cabin on Index Lake. The cabin had been flattened by the earthquake, but the plywood was still usable. With this material we added onto the old trailer. Thank God for friends.

At last we were back on our own land. The next thing we did was start clearing for a garden. We placed the garden in an area near our trailer where there was a natural deposit of dark colored soil. Nearby was a dense stand of alder and large spruce trees. With much hard work we cleared the area and developed a very productive garden. We tried to stick with the organic method as much as possible. Margaret was always careful to share the first fruits from the garden with others. Later I cleared for a much larger garden down by the beaver pond. The lower garden took some time also. The soil was blue clay and had no fertility at all. To take care of this I mixed half sawdust and half horse manure and let it compost for a year in a big pile. This really made it another good garden. In later years Sharon and her husband used the same area for their garden. Sharon is like her mother as she likes her garden.

Until the earthquake the beavers had built up such a dam at the pond that the water was running over Victory Road. I had our mail box nailed to a cottonwood tree below our house and when I went to get the mail one day the beavers had cut the mailbox tree down! Brian and Dan had trapped some of the beavers but the earthquake must have killed the rest of them as they disappeared at that time.

Decisions

By the summer of 1967 we realized we were facing a decision about our income. Fishing with Nick Leman in the summers was a big help, but it took us away from the work of VBC and was not enough to meet our needs. We either needed to seek employment, raise missionary support or continue to fish. None of the above appealed to me at the time. While I will always be thankful for Nick's generosity in allowing us to be involved in his fishing business, this didn't seem like a good option for us.

Going on deputation to raise more missionary income did not appeal to me at all. More and more, I sensed our days of ministering at VBC were about over. I felt we had made a contribution to the camping ministry in the early years there and I am thankful for that opportunity. More helpers were coming for the work and Johnny's son Stan Gillespie and his wife Ginny had come to live at Victory full time as the director.

Both Margaret and I really struggled over what was best to do. What was God's will for us? Margaret came to Alaska to do missionary work and that is what she hoped we could do as a couple. By the end of the 1967 fishing season we had made enough money to make a move. We drove into Anchorage to see a friend, Carl Kroon, who at that time worked for Alaska Sales and Service. We asked Carl if he had a good used car we could afford. Carl introduced us to one of his salesmen, who told us there were only two cars on their whole lot he could recommend, and if he didn't do it Carl would fire him on the spot. With only two cars to choose from it was not too difficult to make the choice. One was a Chevy and the other was a real nice 1965 Pontiac Tempest which we bought, trading in our old 1954 pickup truck. This was a really good buy for us that we could afford. It had low mileage and the car was in excellent condition. With this car we could travel as a family in comfort.

Visiting Family

In 1967 it had been five years since we had been outside to see our family so in late summer we went to California to visit Margaret's parents. While there I contacted Dr. Clyde Narramore, a Christian psychologist, for counseling about what we should do. This was very good for me and I wished I could have stayed longer. Again, money was about to run out and we had to move on. I felt I was just beginning to gain some insight about what we were facing and also other issues that I had been dealing with. I was assured it was not a sin against God to drop our status as missionaries.

With some reluctance we went on to Indiana to see my parents. They were still in good health at that time in their lives and enjoying life. After wondering what to do, we decided to stay with my parents for the winter. They were okay with that as there was room for all of us. It was time for school to start so we sent all three of the children to a nearby grade school in Tunnelton. Brian was in 8th grade, Dan in 6th grade and Sharon was in the 3rd grade. They seemed to adjust to a new school situation. I know Brian and Dan were not too thrilled to spend the winter in Indiana.

We tried to get away as much as possible so as not to put too much strain on my parents. Margaret and my mother got along very well. In later years my father became quieter, while in former years he was actually the life of the party and the biggest cut-up of us all. He was very kind to us all winter. I bought some feeder pigs for the boys to feed during the winter and sell in the spring. This turned out to be a good project for them. For feed we would take my father's pickup truck and glean corn in the fields after harvest. With the five of us it was not long before we had enough corn to last the rest of the year.

I bought some plywood and built a small flat-bottomed boat for the kids to use in the creek below the barn. They spent many hours paddling up and down the creek with their little dog Tippy. Tippy soon caught on when the school bus came each afternoon and he was there to meet the kids as they got off the bus.

In October I got a job at a canning factory in Brownstown, Indiana, firing a steam boiler to process the canning operation. After the canning season was over in November I got a job cutting timber with a local logging contractor. It was not a good paying job, but it met our needs at the time. While in Indiana we attended the White River Baptist Church where my parents were going. I believe it was after an evening church service that Dan told us he didn't want to go to hell, so Margaret led him to the Lord. It was a very real experience for him.

During the last months of 1968 we were all agreed that it was time to head back to Alaska. We rounded up the pigs and with my Father's truck we took them to market. Even after expenses there was a profit. With the pigs sold and other small things taken care of, we headed west to California and then on north. We had told our friends at White River Church we were no longer accepting missionary funds. We did the same with Margaret's home church in San Dimas. We really missed the personal contact with our home churches, though we remained friends.

When we left my parent's home to go back to Alaska I had no idea what we were going to do other than Nick Leman had said we could fish at least one more year with them. So that was what we did the summer of 1968. Also I got the contract of clearing trees for the power line which was to go through our property and on to Victory High School. After clearing the power line right-away for MEA Electric Co-op, we drove to Ninilchik to help Nick in his commercial fishing business for one last year. We are all very thankful to Nick for allowing us to help as it provided for our needs at the time.

The Sawmill

With the proceeds from the sale of our farm I bought a used sawmill and a little Ford tractor. For some time I had thought of buying a sawmill as we had some very good timber on the homestead. Upon locating a used mill near Palmer, I contacted our good friend, Ralph DeVilbiss, who offered the use of his truck to haul the mill home. Ralph even sawed some timbers for me to set the mill on. The sawmill was a pile of junk, but with work it was usable. I had much to learn in operating the mill. A good neighbor, Milo Kimble, helped me with getting the saw blade to run right. With the mill in place we were able to use the spruce and cottonwood trees that were on the homestead. I really enjoyed the logging and sawmill project. In later years I bought timber from the state on the other side of the Matanuska River.

With the mill we were able to saw lumber for Victory Bible Camp to build new cabins. This was a cooperative deal with the camp. Stan would send two or three young men to help saw the logs and at mid-morning the cook at camp, June Radcliff, would come down to the mill with a huge pan of sweet rolls. What a treat!

I am very thankful for the Lord's protection during the years of logging and operating the sawmill because it is a dangerous job. One time as I was sawing, a 2x8 spruce board fell on the saw blade and zipped right by my head. That could have killed me instantly. Then there was the day I was cutting trees down near the river when I sensed something was not right. I looked around and there stood a big, black wolf looking my way. I recognized the wolf as a half tamed animal that our neighbor Marten Vorhies had caught and it had escaped from its pen.

School Bus Driving

When we returned home after the fishing season in 1968, a man by the name of Rick Houston came by looking for a person to drive a school bus for Glacier View School. This turned out to be a good job for us: we could stay on our homestead, help out at camp and operate the sawmill between bus runs. I started driving in the fall of 1968. Little did I know at this time how the bus business would be such a blessing to us as a family and also to others. This was truly from the Lord. All that was required for me to drive was a physical exam and a school bus driving permit. There was no testing for the permit at that time as there is today. With these requirements taken care of, Rick handed me the keys for the bus along with a few words to explain how the bus operated—no extensive driver training was needed back then as there is now. I vividly remember the first day I drove the bus. All went well, but I was so nervous that it gave me a headache.

I soon got used to the routine and looked forward to each day of driving, despite challenges such as winter road conditions and keeping order on the bus. During the winter I would leave home in the dark and it would be dark again by the time I returned from the afternoon route. I remember one day when I stopped at Gunsight Lodge and learned that it was 52 degrees below zero! I'm sure we had the most scenic bus route in the country, with the Chugach Mountains to the south, the Matanuska Glacier and the high treeless tundra where caribou often crossed the highway.

While I was driving the bus and running the sawmill, Margaret was busy with the family, gardening and helping at camp as much as she could.

Jerry and Judy Yates came to Glacier View as teachers in 1969 and continued in that capacity until 1974. They were great teachers and Jerry made my job as a driver much easier, in that he wanted to know if there were any problems on the bus with the kids. When their little daughter, Ginger, was born they asked Margaret if she would take care of her during the school day. She agreed to do this and we really came to love that little girl. Margaret also took care of their son Darrin for a time. Jerry and Judy remain good friends until this day and we were thrilled to learn that they have become believers in Christ.

During their elementary years, all three kids attended Glacier View, which was located near the Cascade Road camp. At that time the school only went through the eighth grade, so each of the kids also attended Victory High School. I am so thankful that all of our children had the privilege of attending VHS. Wally Bays and all the staff were so helpful in the lives of our children.

Dave tilling the Alaska garden.

Margaret holding a prize cauliflower.

Dave sawing a spruce log on his mill.

Dad's Retirement & Home-Going

When my Dad retired in the late sixties, it was the first time he could actually relax and enjoy some recreation. It still amazes me that he could even do this, considering that he was such a workaholic. I look at the way that Dad handled retirement as an example for me that when he could no longer physically handle the work he was content. He and my mother enjoyed some good years until failing health entered in.

On September 3, 1970, my father, Charles A. Lee, went to be with the Lord at the age of 79. Dad had been having light strokes for three years before his home going. After one of the strokes I was called and told that if I wanted to see my father alive I needed to get there in a hurry. So I flew out to see him and got to talk with him. Most of the time he knew me, but would often drift off. One day he said he needed to go out and feed the mules, but of course there were no mules to feed, as they had been sold many years before. We had to put him in a nursing home in Bedford. It was a good home and he was well taken care of there. That was the last time I got to see him alive, as a few months later he passed away.

I was driving the bus at that time, so I had to quickly get a substitute driver. John Hammond came to my rescue just before I flew out for the funeral. Arriving in Indianapolis, a friend from the White River Baptist Church met me for the trip to the farm. However, the airlines lost the suitcase with my good dress suit. Junior Bennet, my driver friend, offered one of his suits as we were near the same size. By the time we went to his home, changed clothes and went on to the funeral home, the service was already started, but at least I got there in time to be with my mother, sister and relatives for the funeral service.

I have always regretted that our children did not get to know my father better when he was in good health. When Dad passed on to be with the Lord, I thought about how I could go on in life with no father to consult. Dad did not talk much, but we had a good relationship and worked well together. I thank God for my earthly parents.

After my father passed away my mother did not want the responsibilities of managing the farm so we transferred ownership from Mother to Donna and me. Later I bought Donna's portion of the farm. Our mother continued to live on the farm until it was not safe for her to be there by herself. Donna and her husband Phil took Mother to their home in Indianapolis where she had a good home until the Lord took her to be with Him.

Donna's daughter Linda and husband, Jerry Norris, lived in California for a while, but wanted to return to Indiana. My mother said they could live in the farm house, so they moved in and fixed up the old house. Later we had some acreage around the house surveyed so they could own the house and some land around it. Several years after Jerry and Linda returned to Indiana, they trusted Christ as Savior and their lives changed dramatically. They continue to follow the Lord and are active in a local church.

Cabin Building

The journey continued with a new venture in 1970. We decided to subdivide some of the homestead and build cabins to sell. I used lumber from the mill to build a small cabin near the sawmill. When it was partly finished a lady named Rosalie Tyler came by and wanted to buy it so she could have a cabin near VBC.

In preparation for the subdivision, I contacted Mr. Earl Barnard, an engineer who had done some work for VBC. Earl surveyed the area and drew up plans. Next we went to Palmer to appear before the platting and zoning board.

Appearing before the platting and zoning board proved to be the most exasperating and frustrating experience that either of us had ever endured. The board invariably would find some detail wrong with the plat. This meant Earl had to go back to the drawing board and the price went up for each change made.

Three times we went before the board with the suggested changes made and still it was not correct according to them. Earl and I talked about what to do next and decided to go before the board one more time with the plat map remaining the same. No changes were made, but to our amazement one man on the board suggested they pass it. With the plat accepted, we got out of their presence in a hurry, hoping never to go before this dictatorial body of unelected bureaucrats again!

As a believer in Christ how did I handle this most trying time through the subdivision process—the disappointments, frustration at the extra work involved, bitterness and even anger? I can remember Earl and I would leave the board meetings just seething with anger. There are many times in my spiritual walk that I have had to go to the throne of Grace confessing my many sins and seeking God's forgiveness. Earl is a fine Christian man and he controlled himself very well. Now after some years have passed it is *almost* laughable to think about the experience.

Once the subdivision was completed and surveyed in 1972, I could sell the lots as needed. With the camp's D8 dozer, I pulled the cabin Rosalie had purchased to the lot she chose, built an outhouse, and made some rather crude shelves and counters so she could use the cabin.

When word got out that I had these lots for sale they were quickly spoken for. This meant much work for me because I would sell each lot with a small cabin and outhouse ready for use. From 1972 to 1974 we sold five of the lots.

In 1975 the director of Victory High School, Cadette Morgan, asked about obtaining some land for Victory Bible Camp. We agreed to sell VBC twenty acres on the hill where TeePee camp was located. We also sold forty acres for the proposed Ranch Camp ministry. We are very blessed to see part of our homestead being used to reach kids for the Lord.

According to my record it was in 1977 that our good friend Vera Parkins contacted me to build a home on one of the lots. It was a larger building than I had done before. This required more time and lumber and some house plan changes. Then, in 1979 Arctic Missions bought tract F from us, including an unfinished house that I was building. While I was working on this house Margaret came to me with a letter from Sharon, who was at Multnomah Bible School. We both sat on a sawhorse reading the long letter telling us about a certain young man she was interested in. We could tell this was a serious relationship with Marlin Beachy. We had no picture or other information on Marlin, but I can remember so clearly the peace the Lord gave us about this young man and we have never been disappointed with Marlin and his wonderful family.

Isn't God good that He can reach into our hearts and minds with His peace and presence? It is so real and comforting. The Lord has blessed us with a wonderful family. All are true born again believers following the Lord.

Bus Contract

I believe it was 1971, when Sharon was 12, that we flew to North Carolina and picked up a new bus for Rick Houston from the factory. On the drive home we went by the farm to get my mother to ride up on the bus with us. Sharon was a happy traveler and my mother certainly enjoyed the trip.

In 1977 Rick Houston informed us that he no longer wanted the bus contract and if I wanted a job I would have to bid on the contract for myself. At first I was not too favorable to the idea as this would be a new venture for us. With much thought and prayer we decided to submit a proposal for the contract as we really needed the income from this business. Rick gave us good advice on how to prepare the paper work to present to the school board. This was a learning process for me to run a business. One problem was that I had no previous experience in this kind of business, which made it difficult to get the required insurance.

After spending much time and many miles traveling to Palmer, Wasilla and Anchorage, I was able to get the insurance from Max Olsen at Pippel Insurance in Palmer. It also took much pencil work to figure out the right amount to cover expenses and make a profit. This was a sealed bid contract, so at the appointed day I showed up at the school district office not knowing if my proposal would be accepted or not. When the time was up and no one else showed up to bid on the Glacier View bus route, my bid was opened and checked out.

The fellow who opened the contract asked if I thought I could make it on what I had put in my bid. I thought I could, but he suggested that since we were the only bidder we should increase the amount submitted. I told him he was the boss and that would be fine with me. We had our first contract and named the business Glacier View

Transportation. This had to be from the Lord since we came back from Indiana with not much prospect for income. God once again came to our rescue.

Through the years, with the sale of lumber and cabins we had saved enough money to buy three very good used buses. As a result we were in business debt free. This gave us a good start on the new venture. One of the buses was the one that I drove up from the factory in North Carolina for Rick.

Those were busy years for all of us with the bus driving, the sawmill, the children in school, and a large garden.

Physical & Spiritual Health

At this period of time we were fortunately all in good health. This was a blessing because we had no health insurance or savings for this need. Again, God was good in allowing us to be healthy. Earlier, while living in the Trapper's cabin, Margaret experienced some seizures after Sharon was born. She got over them in time and had no more problems with seizures the rest of her life.

I thank God that He is faithful to His own, those that He has called to Himself. He says He will keep us strong to the end so that we will be blameless on the day of our Lord Jesus Christ (1 Cor. 1:8-9). God who has called us into fellowship with His Son, our Lord Jesus Christ, is faithful. I can relate to Steve Brown, an evangelist and Bible teacher from Florida, who often said, "I am just a struggling Christian, sometimes victorious and sometimes not." I know I was not as faithful in Bible study and prayer as I should have been but I made it a practice to pray before I started each bus run. I also prayed for our friends and neighbors as I drove along the highway.

I'm sure I was not the spiritual husband, father and leader that I should have been. I am so thankful for a godly wife who maintained a consistent walk with her Lord. She loved God's Word, loved children and taught Sunday school for many years. Margaret was a wonderful help to me and our family. Thanks to her our children are where they are today. Margaret was outgoing. For many years it was a rare Sunday that we did not have people in for dinner after church.

I remember the times when our good friends Ernie and Caroline Lucia came out from Anchorage for Thanksgiving dinner. This was a great time for all of us. Our kids and theirs got along very well and enjoyed the outdoor activities. I remember one Thanksgiving in particular because it snowed three feet and we were afraid that no one could get up Victory Road to our house. After much struggle everyone arrived safely and a great time was had by all.

For the most part those were good years through the seventies. We were back in Alaska in our own home (such as it was), together as a family. It had been my desire that if I ever did get married and have a family that we could always be together as a family. I'm sure this idea came from growing up on the farm where we all lived and worked together. God has been good in allowing me this blessing.

I had work near at hand to meet family needs with the bus driving job, the saw mill and other projects. But with all of this that God had provided for us, I still missed the farm life. I can remember so well how I struggled with this issue. Was I in disobedience to God's will for us, for me to continue to have this desire to be back on the farm? When we sold our farm in 1964 I told the Lord I was willing to go back to Alaska as a family. I know I was sincere when I told Him that, so why did I not have peace about this question? One thing for sure, divorce was not given any thought.

At times I would just walk for miles because of the frustration I felt over this issue. Despite those feelings, I did enjoy hiking the many miles of mountain trails seeing the birds, animals and wild flowers. Alaska is a great and beautiful land so why couldn't I be satisfied and happy here? I know if I had not brought the family back to Alaska, Brian and Dan would have been very unhappy, for this was the land they loved. I am not saying I agonized all day long every day over this question because we did have a good life with many blessings from the Lord, but the thought was much on my mind.

In life on our spiritual journey we face times when a change must be made and a decision is required. In our family I made the best judgment that I could think of and that was for us to be back in Alaska. I did not regret making this decision, but continued to struggle with the lingering thought that I wasn't in the right place.

Hunting Stories

In the fall of 1966 I got the urge to go sheep hunting. With a pack, a sandwich and a .300H&H Winchester rifle, I set off on the trail on the west side of Packsaddle Creek. This is a good trail, but very steep in places. My plan was to follow the trail to Anthracite Ridge, go behind Victory Peak and down to the canyon to the Hicks Creek trail that leads to Index Lake. It is a good one day hike and I have done it a number of times, back when I was much younger.

As I worked my way along I kept looking for sheep. About halfway down the ridge I spotted a white object a long way off, not too far above the Hicks Creek trail. When I checked with field glasses it turned out to be a huge ram, much lower in elevation that sheep usually range, and close to the trail that I planned to take. The question was how to get close enough to get a shot at him. Moving as cautiously as I could, I made my way down the ridge and into the canyon, where I was out of his sight. Once on the trail I proceeded to where I thought he was. As I stood up to look, the ram also stood up, so I fired off a quick shot and down he went. This ram was really a beauty. There was no way I could pack this big fellow, horns and all, so I took two trips to pack him home.

The horns ended up having quite a history. While we were in Indiana one time they disappeared, but our friend Vera Parkins said she knew where they were. She was able to get them back for us. Eventually, at the urging of some of our friends, we had them mounted with a full head mount. We hung this in the living room, and one day the mount fell off the wall, bounced off the ironing board and rolled across the floor, scaring Margaret out of her wits. The horns are now at Brian's house.

Sometime around 1972 I decided a horse would be useful. I bought a horse from our neighbor, Marilyn Meekin, along with a saddle and bridle. Bess was a sound horse that we could ride or use to pack gear. I soon discovered there were two things I had to be careful about: she was hard to shoe and was afraid of vehicles. Another neighbor, Ed Stevenson, helped with shoeing. We had to throw her to the ground, tie up her feet, and hold her head down. Eventually she improved to where I could pick up her feet to check her hooves. As for the cars, I learned to really hang on when one went by!

I went on a number of hunting trips, but a few of them stand out. One fall our friend Jim Edmonds and I decided to go on a moose hunt across the Matanuska River. Jim had a horse named Duchess and I took Bess, and Dan went with us. On the other side of the river, we were walking along, leading our horses when we saw a coyote running through the brush. Jim quickly shot at the coyote, causing Duchess to bolt. She took off downriver in high gear, with Jim's sleeping bag and supplies. Usually we could hardly get that old nag out of a slow walk. We looked around for some time, but Duchess was long gone. Jim went back home to get help and eventually found the horse quietly eating, several miles from where she left us.

Meanwhile, Dan and I had to decide what to do after this unexpected situation. We chose to continue the hunt, so we set up camp—which amounted to finding a good spot to lay out our sleeping bags. The next day we started up the mountain and climbed above the tree line so that we could look down on any moose that might show up. Sure enough, we saw a really nice moose. While figuring out how to get a little closer for a shot, we happened to look up the mountain above us, where we saw some goats. Since I had never shot a goat before, we headed up to where the animals were, which was much lower than they usually feed. I ended up getting three goats. Somehow I broke my hunting knife, so I skinned the goats with a broken knife.

We rounded up Bess, loaded the meat on the packsaddle and started home. Coming to the river, we discovered the water was deeper than the day before, because of warmer temperatures thawing the glacier ice. Bess was a good mountain horse and not afraid of water. I put Dan on top of the meat on the packsaddle and started across. Partway through we got into something like quicksand. At this, Bess really went to work, plunging and plowing through the water. I had started out leading her, but she soon got ahead of me. As she went by, I grabbed her tail and she pulled me through. Dan hung on for dear life and I got soaked, but fortunately we were okay. We made it home safely and the meat was really good.

One year John Gillespie had a good friend visit him at VBC, who got the notion to go on a sheep hunt. Johnny asked me to go along and he asked Ed Stevenson to take us in with his horses. We started on the Pinochle Trail, went up through the pass, then west across Hicks Creek into a valley to what we always called the "Forks". We set up camp—first class compared to what I was used to—with horses, a nice tent, good equipment and plenty of food. I usually carried a light pack, slept on the ground and brought very little food when I hunted.

The next day we could see sheep high up near the top of the mountain behind us. Johnny's friend was an older man and appeared to not be in good physical condition. Before we attempted to go for the sheep, I asked him if he thought he could climb up near them. When he admitted that he had a heart problem, I was not about to take him up the mountain. It was tempting, but we just watched them through a spotting scope.

Our camp was in a really nice spot and the weather was good. There were caribou all around us so I asked the fellow if he would like to shoot one. We found a small band of nice caribou and he promptly shot one. He seemed happy with the hunt even if he didn't get to shoot a sheep, and I enjoyed seeing all the animals.

After returning home, he had a few days left in his stay and wanted to shoot a black bear. I didn't have time for another hunt, so I told him to go to the garbage dump, where people often saw bears. He was gone hardly any time and came back all excited, saying he had shot a bear. Sure enough, he had shot the biggest black bear I had ever seen! I used my tractor loader to hoist it up and take it to the camp shop to dress it out.

Another time, our friend Pogie Parkins wanted to shoot a black bear. One day I spotted a bear on Hicks Mountain, so Pogie and I drove to Hicks Creek. From there we hiked up the mountain. It didn't take long to get to where we saw the bear, slowly feeding his way along the slope. Bears don't linger long in one area; they just keep moving. We got to within about eighty yards below the bear. I told Pogie to shoot but he just stood there with his gun in his hands, watching the bear. He just couldn't seem to pull the trigger. I waited as long as I dared, then went ahead and shot the bear. Pogie didn't say anything for a while, but I don't think he was disappointed that I shot it. We dressed it out and took the meat and hide home. Bear meat is good to eat, so we didn't waste any of the animal.

One other time I went sheep hunting with a fellow named Frank Robertson. Frank was an older man who was working at VBC at the time. We started at the camp dining hall and took the trail along the north side of Index Lake. We followed this trail from the lake, along the rim of Hicks Creek canyon then on to the lower end of Anthracite Ridge, which is quite a bit of a climb. I finally spotted a band of rams that I thought we could get near. By this time Frank was getting very thirsty, so I told him to stay put while I found some water. It didn't take long to find a little spring and soon Frank was okay. The rams were still in sight, so I suggested that we climb a little closer. Frank chose to stay there so he wouldn't scare the sheep. I found a good position to shoot from and dropped a ram with one shot. Frank re-joined me, I cut up the sheep, we loaded our packs and set out for home. With loaded packs it was slower going, so that by the time we got to Index Lake it was dark. We sat down to take a much needed rest and heard rustling in the leaves on the hill above us. I had visions of a bear coming upon us because of the sheep meat in our packs, so I had the rifle ready. Fortunately it was just a porcupine that walked right by our feet. We made it home safely in spite of the dark.

My last sheep hunt ended up having some exciting moments. A good friend, Dave Lazer, joined me on this excursion. We packed our gear onto his horse and hiked up the mountain behind our home. The trail we followed has a very steep portion near the spring where we get our water. When the horse came to this spot he started lunging, in an attempt to climb the hill. After a few lunges, he rose up so high that he toppled over backward! He rolled off the trail into some trees, with his feet uphill. He lay there, without struggling, since he couldn't get his feet underneath his body.

We removed the packsaddle and supplies and cut away some trees that were below the horse, so we could roll him over. As soon as he felt his feet touch the ground he got right up. Thankfully, there didn't seem to be any damage, so we repacked our gear and proceeded on our way.

After a while we came to what we call the "boulder field", an area below Victory Peak filled with huge boulders from the mountain. There is no trail through it and it is a difficult area to cross. By the time we got through that and up to the pass between Victory Peak and Anthracite Ridge, it was getting late, so we set up a simple camp for the night.

In the morning I rose early and spotted a band of rams on the north side of Anthracite Ridge. After watching them awhile, we saw that there was no way to approach the rams without them seeing us. Dave decided to hike way out around the sheep so he could come from behind and head them my direction.

While Dave hiked, I sat on a small knob in a chilly wind. His idea worked and the rams started to move toward me. Despite shaking from cold, I was able to shoot one of the rams when they came near. I was thankful it didn't roll off the narrow trail, as it could have fallen several hundred feet. Even so, I had to hold onto the ram with one hand while field dressing it, to keep it from rolling away. When Dave returned we finished preparing the sheep, then packed up and returned home by a better trail.

Hunting was one activity I enjoyed, both as a means to provide for our family, and to see the beautiful creation that God has made. Colossians 3:17 tells us "that whatever we do, do it as unto the Lord." So even hunting can be done for the Lord if we recognize Him as the provider and see His hand in creation. Praise the Lord for his creation we can enjoy and use for our needs.

Our Children—Our Blessings

Brian and Dan loved the lifestyle we lived in the mountains where they learned to hunt, trap and fish. About their late elementary years, the boys began trapping on the homestead for rabbits and other animals. When Marv and Linda DenBleyker and family moved to the area, their son Mike wanted to trap also. Some hunting competition caused friction between the boys. We had to call a father's meeting to settle the issue. As Brian and Dan looked at it, they were here first so they had first rights. We fathers suggested the boys establish certain areas for each person since there was plenty of room for each one at that time. Dan said that they all laugh about the trap line problem now.

The boys were always the adventurous types and took advantage of any hunting trip. One early August day I decided we needed some fresh caribou meat. I knew some caribou ranged in the hills above Hicks Creek and from previous experiences knew these bulls were fat and in good shape before the breeding season. So Brian, Dan and I hiked back to "the Forks" and camped out for the night.

From the pass we hiked west down across Hicks Creek and up to the treeless hills where we spotted a band of caribou bulls. We got up to easy shooting distance just as the clouds rolled in. I didn't think much about the threatening weather so I shot a nice bull. By this time it was starting to snow, but I proceeded to dress out the downed animal. By the time I finished it was really snowing hard and stacking up on the ground. The boys were beginning to get wet and cold. We packed the meat down to the Hicks Creek crossing. There I built a big fire as there was a good supply of dry spruce wood. The boys got warmed up while I hung the meat high up in a spruce tree. It was summer weather when we left home and the boys were in their tennis shoes. This was early August and the leaves were still on the trees.

The snow kept piling up until there was at least eight inches on the ground. We were not prepared to spend the night there so I put a good eighty pounds of meat in my pack and we took off for the highway. The boys had wet feet because those tennis shoes were not waterproof. I was plenty warm with the load on my back. We waded through the snow getting out to the highway and our truck. I know the boys were glad to get out of the snow and get their feet dried out.

One week later I went back to get the meat I had hung up in a spruce tree, fully expecting the meat to be spoiled because the weather had turned warm again. When I took it down it looked terrible—all black and crusty. But to my surprise when I cut into the meat it was in perfect condition. This was fully aged meat and some of the best tasting game I have ever eaten.

I am very pleased with how well our children did in school. It was one of my concerns that they would have the fear that I had in school, especially high school. Thankfully this never happened. I recognize that I was not as supportive of them in school endeavors as I should have been. Margaret was faithful to attend the various school activities to encourage our children.

Brian graduated from Victory High School in 1972 and then went on to Multnomah Bible School in Portland, Oregon and later to Montana Institute of the Bible. At a young age he showed leadership ability and did well in school. I remember one year, probably eighth grade, when he went to a spelling bee. He did well until the word "cello" tripped him up. He continued to learn and grow in Christ during high school, with involvement in gospel teams and sports.

Dan also attended Victory High School. He did well in school and was active in sports and other interests. I think he made a name for himself while in school with his pranks and jokes. I remember the time Dan came in from school saying he had something he wanted to talk to us about. Dan confessed that he and a buddy had been caught smoking cigars on school property. We could tell that Dan really felt sorry for his misdeeds. We accepted his forgiveness and no more was said to him, but we had an inward chuckle about it.

In 1974 Dan graduated from high school and went on to Multnomah for one year of Bible classes. One year was enough for Dan. He preferred being outdoors in the wilderness.

During their young adult years the boys were involved in many adventurous activities, including the sport of kayaking. Lee Althens was also in on this activity on some of the local rivers. One fall Brian and Dan parked their kayaks near the saw-mill. Later, as I was plowing snow with the bulldozer I wiped out the kayaks and that was the end of that sport. I had completely forgotten they were by the mill when I needed to clear the snow.

Shortly after high school Brian and Dan decided they wanted to move out, so they built a small one-room log cabin among the spruce trees near the sawmill. That was fine with us and showed initiative on their part. As Dan said, they were not so far away, but what they could come home for a meal. One day Dan reported that he was getting really tired of pancakes every morning. This was a good learning time in their lives, building the cabin, learning to cook and obtaining other skills in the process. They had a problem with mice moving into the cabin. One day Dan came to us all disgusted because a mouse had built a nest in one of his good shirt sleeves and eaten a hole in it.

At this time Brian and Dan were commercial fishing with their uncle, Nick Leman. Fishing gave them a good income and the means for their activities and schooling. They also started working for a neighbor, Eldon Reese, as Big Game hunting guides. They got into the sawmill business as well, when they bought a Mobile Dimension sawmill in Portland, Oregon along with a truck to haul the mill home. The boys had used my old sawmill until it just wore out and could no longer be used. This old sawmill is among the "heirloom" pieces of equipment we have in our possession.

Sharon, our daughter and the youngest child with her big smile, is such a blessing to us. When Sharon was just a toddler she had no appetite and looked frail. Our good doctor and friend, Jim Pinneo, said there was nothing wrong with her, she just had to start eating. The first year in grade school Sharon came home one afternoon and announced that her teacher told her she had to eat all her lunch, so she did start to eat more. Rather timid at first in school, Sharon overcame this challenge and went on to do well.

I remember that, as a student at Victory High School, Sharon stood out because of her height and fair skin among the Alaska native students. She was active in sports and gospel team ministry. She graduated from high school in 1977 and went on to Multnomah School of the Bible for three years, graduating in 1980.

Sharon kept occupied during the summer months between school semesters, doing odd jobs such as painting cabins and the bus barn. After her second year at Multnomah she went to a Bible camp in Montana as a counselor. When we went to the airport to get Sharon we did not recognize her as she was so tanned, with sun-bleached hair from being outdoors in a warmer climate. The following summer after graduation, she spent six weeks in Guatemala on a mission training trip.

I remember one Christmas we went to the airport to pick up Brian as he was coming home from Bible School in Montana and Sharon from Multnomah. While waiting for the two of them, Dan showed up from a big game guiding trip on Kodiak Island. So we collected all three kids on one trip to town. What a happy time it was for us with each one sharing their experiences of the past few months. There were many trips to the airport during those college years. Again I can't help but lift up a prayer of thanksgiving to God for giving us this family. I was so encouraged to see each one go on to college and training for their future lives.

Thinking Back

I praise the Lord, our God, for blessing us with a godly family. Before God called me to Himself I despaired of ever having a wife or family. I was very shy around the young ladies, so had no girlfriend or even close friends. One thought I had was that if by some chance a young lady took notice of me, there must be something wrong with her! So with that mindset it would have been a disaster for both of us had I married at that time in my life.

In thinking back to when I lived at home on the farm, our good neighbors, the John Sherfick family, had a daughter growing up into a very attractive young lady. John and I were good friends and we helped each other on our farms so I got to know Mary Ethel very well. I know now when I think back to that time that my mother and Mary's mother made some attempts to get us together. My mother would have Mary come to our home to help with the house work. I'm sure my mother was in very good health and did not need that much help. While she was there I would ask Mary to help me with the hogs or other projects on the farm. She was a willing worker and a good helper, but still a teenager and I was nearing 30. At the same time I was having serious periods of depression. This is when God in His great mercy and loving kindness moved me and crowded me to Himself in Alaska. I did not go off to Alaska because of lost love; Mary and I were just good friends. I believe in God's sovereignty, that in His grace and mercy He did not allow my relationship with Mary to go any further than it did.

I thank God He transformed my life and gave me a wife and family. I recall so many times 2 Corinthians 5:17, the very first verse the Lord gave me when I started to read the little New Testament that my godly mother insisted I take with me when I left home in 1951. Margaret, the wife God gave me, was a wonderful person and helpmeet. As I write these pages I wish she was here to help me with spelling and proper sentence structure. I admired her educational achievements at college and Bible School.

The Farm Purchase

As believers in Christ, called aliens and strangers, we continue our journeys in this present world, at times with great blessings and sometimes with painful trials—sometimes with discouragement and in conflicts and testing. I am reminded many times of I Peter 4:12 which was a verse the Lord gave me when I was experiencing things in my life that were indeed painful and strange. Praise the Lord for the comfort of His Word.

Early in the year of 1978 I received an unexpected phone call from a cousin's son, Mark Fields, informing me that he was about to lose his farm. This was the farm that my Field's grandparents owned while I was growing up. Mark wanted to know if I would like to buy his interest in it. I was indeed interested in the farm, but when Mark told me how much he owed there was no way I could think of paying that much— $240,000. I informed him that the best thing for both of us was for him to sell his equipment, the Harvestore silo and related items. If he would do this I would like to see about buying the land.

We made many phone calls over the next few weeks, but no agreement was made on the price of the farm. Mark did go ahead and sell off the silo and other equipment. At this time I decided I would fly out to see if it were possible for us to buy the farm. Mark had financed the farm through the Federal Land Bank so I drove over to Salem to the Land Bank office to see an agent about the farm. No agreement was made so I went back to Alaska to wait for further developments regarding our negotiations.

After a few months, Margaret and I flew out for more talks. Finally Mark and I went to the Bank in Medora where we both had accounts and knew the bank president, Russell Sherrell. Thanks to Russell we came to agree on a price for us to buy the farm. With this settled, Margaret and I again went to the Federal Land Bank in Salem to see about financing. After some time in discussing the terms we financed $96,000 to buy the farm. This was a huge amount for us. I did not have any money for a down payment and just had to finance the whole amount. For security it was the farm itself plus other land we owned in Indiana. None of our Alaska land was involved in this deal.

As a young person I dreamed of owning this farm if it ever came up for sale. My grandparents owned the farm and lived there until they died. In fact this land has been in the family for over one hundred years so it is something like an heirloom farm. During the time we were in the process of buying the farm, another cousin, Paul, offered sound advice— if I did not buy the farm I would always regret not doing so. I think he was right even though at the time that much debt didn't feel too good. With the financing settled, Margaret and I went back to Alaska. We were depending on the bus business to help pay for the farm. As it turned out we were able to make substantial payments over the next four years, cutting the amount owed nearly in half.

When Margaret and I flew back to Indiana in the summer of 1979 we received a rude surprise. While I thought we had all things settled and in order for purchasing the farm, Mark had, without notifying us, sold the timber to Gerry Brock in Leesville. Gerry and his crew were clear-cutting the timber off the farm as we arrived. I was disappointed and angry with Mark for this deal. I immediately went to Gerry Brock to see what I could do about the trees. I asked what he would take for the remaining trees that were left. Gerry said the price was $6,000, so I wrote out a check for that amount to save what was left of the trees.

Because of Mark's loss we were able to buy the farm and, despite those circumstances, I am thankful to the Lord for this opportunity. I feel that as a land owner, we are stewards of God's creation. Mark's father, my cousin Leonard, was a retired steam fitter and had his own farm to enjoy. We often talked about our farms and wondered if we thought more of the land than serving the Lord. My prayer was and still is that I would never allow house, land, equipment and things of the world to take me from serving the Lord. I still remember that fateful day back in 1951 when I went to the barn to go to work and realized that these things I had worked so hard for did not bring the joy and peace that I thought they would. Praise God He crowded me to Himself—as it says in Ephesians 1:4, God chose us.

Weddings

The decade of the eighties was a very busy and exciting time, as well as challenging. All three children entered into marriage relationships. Dan and Kathy were the first, getting married March 29, 1980, at Victory Bible Camp. The first time we really noticed Kathy Alderman was when someone asked if we had observed Dan and Kathy sitting together in church. We soon saw they were interested in one another and we began to get acquainted with this young lady. Kathy proved to be a very nice, friendly, godly person. She was working at Victory Bible Camp at the time and lived next door to us with another young lady. It sometimes amazed me that Kathy accepted us as we were. She would often pop in to visit or play board games, and became like another daughter to us. Kathy sewed her wedding dress at our house and did a lovely job. Her parents and brothers came up from South Carolina for the wedding. Kathy had a fine family and we enjoyed getting acquainted with Rev. Dick and Martha Alderman.

After Dan and Kathy married they lived in the little log cabin that Brian and Dan had built. In the fall of 1980 Dan was working for Hal Alward as a hunting guide. Kathy stayed home but was planning to fly to the hunting camp after it was set up, to cook for the men. However, on September 1 she hopped on a flight to surprise Dan, and in the sovereignty of God, both she and the pilot were killed in a crash. It was so devastating, so hard to comprehend, but we turned to the Lord in our grief and He gave us peace even through our tears. I had never realized before how much it hurt to have a loved one die in such a sudden and tragic way. We knew Kathy was in heaven with the Lord she loved and, because of our hope in Christ, we know that someday we will see her again. A week after Kathy's death we had a memorial service for her and a burial on a portion of our homestead. We sensed the Lord's presence with us throughout this painful time, and we are also thankful for kind friends who were so supportive and helpful.

• • •

The next family member to announce intentions for marriage was Brian. Theirs was another Victory Bible Camp romance! Lori Althens and her brother Lee, had come to Alaska from New Hampshire. Both of them worked at VBC for a time, and Lori also attended Moody Bible Institute. Brian and Lori's relationship grew over a period of a couple years while both of them were in school, as well as in Alaska.

Their wedding ceremony was performed August, 30, 1980 on the family farm in New Hampshire, which is also the location that Lori's parents were married. They had a beautiful outdoor wedding. My sister and mother went to their wedding and I am thankful that they represented our family. Brian is our firstborn son and I am proud of him, his love for the Lord and his family. Lori is a beautiful, godly wife for Brian and I admire her dedication to their family as well as her service for the Lord.

After Brian and Lori married, they settled on the acreage Brian chose earlier from our homestead. In the early years they worked in Ninilchik at Nick Leman's fishing sites, but later they bought their own drift boat and began fishing in Prince William Sound. They also lived in Cantwell for a time, where Brian served as pastor of Cantwell Bible Church.

Several years later they adopted Travis Wayne, who was born in Idaho on March 22, 1988. Two years later they were blessed with Chelsea Dawn, born to them on June 8, 1990. What a blessing that God has given us grandchildren, and that they are being raised in godly homes.

• • •

During Sharon's last year at Multnomah Bible School she met a young man named Marlin Beachy, whom she grew to be good friends with. After graduating from Multnomah in 1980, Sharon stayed in Portland with friends, Tom and Susan Raymond, and worked at a Christian day care. I mentioned earlier about the letter Sharon wrote to us telling about Marlin and the peace the Lord gave us about their relationship. So when Marlin came to ask for Sharon, we were happy to give our permission and blessing.

Sharon and Marlin were married December 19, 1981 at Victory Bible Camp. The wedding was a happy day for all of us. Marlin's parents flew from Ohio for this special occasion. After the wedding they went back to Portland for Marlin to finish his last semester at Multnomah. In the summer of 1982 they fished in Ninilchik with Brian and Lori, then moved to Ohio to be near Marlin's parents and take additional college classes. Marlin told me he would like to live in Alaska for a while where Sharon had grown up, so he could get acquainted with us, the people and the area. In 1983 they moved back to Alaska and have been here ever since. I promptly put Marlin to work driving a school bus for us.

Marlin continued to commercial fish for a few summers, then worked with Dan in gold mining for two summers. Their son Ryan Eric, our first grandchild, was born March 30, 1984. During this time the local church didn't have a pastor and Marlin was one of the men who preached. After a couple years the church leaders asked him to be the pastor. So on November 8, 1986, the day their daughter Melissa Ruth was born, Marlin officially became the pastor of Victory Community Church. He was still driving a school bus as well, and in 1986 I brought Marlin and Lee Althens into the business as partners. Later I got out of the business entirely and Lee and Marlin have had the bus business ever since. Marlin and Sharon had their third child, Rachel Deanna, on November 15, 1989.

• • •

Four years after Kathy's home-going, Dan was introduced to a young lady in Seward, Sandy Adrian. A mutual friend gave Dan her number, hoping he would respond with a call to Sandy. Dan did call her, but did not expect much from the contact. As Dan tells the story, they talked for some time, then decided to meet in Anchorage at a restaurant. From the very first meeting they enjoyed each other's company. It was close to being "love at first sight". They had a lot in common and were both recovering from previous marriages. Soon they realized this was of the Lord and were married in Seward on November 13, 1984, with a few close friends in attendance.

After a few years they desired to have children. In God's sovereignty He chose to bless them with children through adoption. First to come was Jeffrey David, born November 19, 1989, just a few days after Rachel. Their next special delivery was Jesse Tyler, born July 20, 1993. For their next little blessing, Dan and Sandy traveled to China to pick up Jennifer Katherine, who was born on February, 12, 1995. My observation is that they have done a wonderful job in raising their family in a Christ-like way.

I thank the Lord that He has blessed us with such a wonderful family with our three children and eight grandchildren. Each one is a special and unique person.

It was our desire for our children to have some of the land from our homestead. Brian and Dan chose a tract for their home sites that contains about twenty-four acres, so each one has approximately twelve acres of homestead land. Both of them built very attractive log homes overlooking the Matanuska River and the Chugach Mountain Range. The view is fantastic and with their spotting scopes they can watch for moose and bears on the mountains across the river.

Marlin and Sharon chose a tract just off Victory Road for their acreage. This plot contained the most level land on the homestead, except for the forty acres sold to Victory Bible Camp. In earlier years Margaret and I had developed a large garden on this tract and Marlin and Sharon have continued using the garden. This land has been such a blessing from the Lord

Celebrating the twenty-fifth anniversary.

Enjoying the grandchildren—Margaret holding Melissa, Dave holding
Travis, and Ryan sitting on the floor.

Trips To The Farm

Through the years there was a lot of travel by plane, truck and car to the farm in Indiana. I have already mentioned our experiences traveling the Alcan Highway in the early years. In 1981 we bought a used F250 Ford pickup truck. John Hammond loaned us a camper shell that his father had made and which just fit the truck.

During the eighties and nineties we traveled back and forth numerous times. The first year we traveled with the truck was in July, 1982. Along the way we visited with friends in various places. After spending time at the farm that summer, we headed home on September 11. The Lord was with us all the way. As we traveled along Margaret kept an account of expenses in a book we carried with us. She would also add comments about what we saw along the way. I don't think Margaret was especially fond of the long trips, but she never complained.

We made summer trips in 1983, '85, '86 and '88. In 1990 we left Alaska in March and stayed in Indiana for two years. When we returned to Alaska in 1992, my cousin, Leonard Fields, joined us. Leonard was just like a kid, he was so happy for this new experience. Weeks before, we had purchased an almost new Crown Victoria Ford car from our neighbor, Fern McKeaigg, for easier traveling. At first Margaret said, "What will people think when they see us driving this nice car?" I replied, "Margaret, all of our married life we have been driving around in old cars and pickups, so why can't we enjoy a really good car for a change!" She did adjust to our new car in due time. The car had low mileage, 42,000 and was in immaculate condition—even smelled new.

We travelled the usual route north to Alaska, arriving in Dawson Creek, B.C. where we stopped for most of a day, enjoying the sights. This was the 50th anniversary year of the opening of the Alaska Highway.

After arriving at home, Brian took Leonard and me on his fishing boat for two days. Then Marlin took us up to Dan's gold mine. This was a wonderful time for all of us. Leonard flew home and Margaret and I drove back to Indiana in September.

Through the 90's we continued to travel back and forth. One memorable trip was the year 1999 when we drove a Honda Accord that I bought from John Gillespie. Marlin helped drive this time. For most of the way we set the cruise control at 70 and away we went. We made good time, getting to the farm in just four days. It usually took us at least six days to make the same trip. Margaret was a good traveler and never complained as she rode along in the back of the car. When asked how she was doing, she replied, "Keep on driving"!

I really enjoyed the many trips, plus they made it possible for us to spend some time on the farm. We really had two homes, one in Alaska and the other on the Indiana farm. I must admit I feel most at home down on the farm. We have always been thankful to the Lord for His protection as we traveled so many miles. It was interesting to note how the road improved over the years; it is now a very good, paved road for most of the distance.

Lee Subdivision #2—1986

By 1986 I was often being asked about land for sale along Victory Road, so we decided to add more lots for sale. I called our friend, Earl Barnard, the engineer to see if he could help us out again. Earl came out to see what we wanted to do and did the preliminary surveying for the proposed addition. This began the whole process again of taking the subdivision plans before the platting and zoning board. We experienced the same frustration, with repeated appearances, hoping we could get their approval. There is no need to record in detail the number of trips, the delays and other problems associated with this appeal for the addition. Finally, much to our relief, they granted their approval on October 22, 1986.

Tim and Sue Gillespie purchased half of tract D, a larger parcel on subdivision #1. Tim is one of Johnny and Nadine's sons. Pat and Nancy Cohen bought Lot # 4 and we supplied lumber for a house. Pat and Nancy are longtime friends who are missionaries with Wycliffe Translators. They worked for over forty years in Vietnam and other countries of Southeast Asia. Robert Gilmore contacted us about the small tract on the south side of the Glenn Highway. This parcel was part of our homestead, but it was so small it was of no practical use for us. Andy and Vi Jensen purchased Lot # 2. Andy and Vi were good friends who served with Victory Bible Camp for a number of years.

The local church chose Lot # 1 in 1988 for a building. Margaret and I agreed to give the lot to the church and we were happy to help in this way. Several men from the church fellowship went across the Matanuska River and cut trees to be sawed for the building. Some men cut the trees, while others hauled the logs to the mill. I sawed the logs into lumber at our saw mill. The men also did the labor of constructing the building, which was then named Spring Creek Bible Church. Years later when the fellowship outgrew this facility, a new church building was constructed at Mile 99 on the Glenn Highway and the name changed to Glacier View Bible Church.

In October, 1989, Lee and Suzie Althens bought Lot # 3. Lee built a bus garage and shop on this property. Later they added an apartment onto the garage, where they now live. Several friends and I helped Lee erect the massive frame for the garage. It was such a strain on all of us that it caused me to have a hernia that had to be repaired. Jeff and Karen Kovac bought Lot # 5. There was no building on the lot, so Jeff bought the little cabin I had sold to Rosalie Tyler years before and moved it down Victory Road to the site. This was the last of the subdivision lots, so I no longer own property in Alaska.

Panic Attacks

During the year of 1989 I started having panic attacks, though I didn't know that was the problem at the beginning. The first time this happened I was at home on a Sunday afternoon. I was not hurting, nor sick or dizzy but just didn't feel right. When I went to bed for the night my heart started beating at a rapid pace. Thinking I might be having a heart attack, I called Brian. He took me to the Emergency Room at the Palmer Hospital. The doctor could not find anything wrong so we went home.

These attacks continued with repeated trips to the hospital. I was given many tests to check my heart, but each time it wasn't a heart attack. The last time, as I was going in by ambulance, I thought, "I must be dying." My heart was wild and doing strange things. I was not scared, but wondered what it might be like to die. At the ER they again gave me all the tests they give a patient in case it is a heart attack. The doctor told me that I couldn't be having a heart attack because my heart was all right. He told me it was panic attacks and gave me a drug to calm me down. The drug gave me relief and I slept in the hospital for the night.

The next morning Dan took me to Charter North Hospital in Anchorage. I was checked in and placed in a room with one other fellow. My roommate was a messy housekeeper but otherwise we got along very well. With medication, and understanding what was going on, I began to feel much better.

This was quite an experience, being in that hospital with all kinds of people and their problems. We had group meetings where we were encouraged to tell all. I was treated well and they even baked a cake for me on my birthday. We had time to read, relax and do other activities between sessions. This was a unique group of human beings with their problems and desires. I felt sorry for the young stripper girls who obviously were leading a hard life. One girl told how she wanted to get training for a better life. I sure hope she did.

Retirement

In 1986 Marlin Beachy and Lee Althens joined me in the bus business, then in 1991 they took over completely. Though officially "retired" I continued working. After selling the bus business to Marlin and Lee, and collecting retirement benefits, I was free to spend more time on the farm. Lord willing, I plan on working as long as strength permits.

Margaret and I enjoyed the opportunity to make many improvements on the farm. After my father could no longer physically manage the farm and keep things repaired, things went downhill, so a lot of repair work had to be done. I had field tile installed to drain off excess water, making the crop fields easier to farm. In 1999 I bought a D-6 Caterpillar dozer. This machine has helped me around the farm to clear fence rows, do stream bank work, shape water ways and do other numerous jobs. At one point I received a "River Friendly Farmer" award for planting trees along the creek bank for erosion control. We planted a small orchard of apple, pear, peach, and cherry trees for home use. We have really enjoyed the fruit over the years. For several years we also had a large garden. Margaret loved the garden project. I'm thankful to the Lord for the years He gave us to work on the improvements that were needed.

It just seemed that the farm was where I belonged. Margaret was happy with the 1965 12 ft. X 55 ft. house trailer we bought in November of 1982 and placed on what had been the Field's farm. It was clean with all new carpet throughout. Buying the trailer was the first thing we did in order for us to have housing on the farm. The old house was no longer usable and it was torn down.

Grandfather Lee's Farm

In June, 1988 I went to the State Bank of Medora on business. While there I inquired about the farm that once belonged to my Grandfather Lee. I knew it had changed hands and was now in default to the bank. I also knew Denny Wayman, the bank branch president, pretty well. I asked Denny about the farm and how much they were asking for it and he said $54,000 for the ninety two acre farm. That was too much for me, but I told him I could give him $36,000 for the farm. As soon as I said the price, Denny said, "sold"! Was I ever surprised with that turn of events! I wrote out a check for $10,000 and signed a contract for the remainder.

I was pleased that I could buy the farm back. It had been given to my grandfather when he and Grandmother Lee were married. They took good care of the place and lived there until they died. At their death my Uncle Ross and Aunt Gertrude bought the farm and when they died it went up for sale. A neighbor, Howard Meyers, bought it. When Howard and his wife, Helen wanted to sell I bought the farm for the first time.

This is the place that Margaret was so unhappy with, especially the house. Because she was unhappy there I sold it to Merle Meyers, who was a retired farmer and just wanted a smaller place to live. A near neighbor, Carl Ratcliff, wanted to buy the place and kept bugging Merle about selling it. Merle told me later that he quoted a high price just to get rid of Carl. But to his surprise, Carl said he would take it, so Merle kept his word and regretfully sold the farm.

The next change came when Carl ended up in jail, losing everything, so the Medora Bank had it. I first bought the farm for $5,500, sold it to Merle for $6,500 and then bought it back again for $36,000!

So on June 9, 1988 it became ours for the second time. Since Margaret didn't have to live in the old house it was fine with her.

That same year I had new siding put on the barn. Around 1980 I bought a new sawmill and planer. With that equipment I could saw some of the oak and other trees that had blown down on the farm. Turning those heavy oak logs on the saw mill caused me to have another hernia and subsequent operation, which was not so good.

Reviewing Life, Renewing Friendships

1980 to 1990 was busy for all of us. Our children were moving out on their own, going to school, getting married and starting families. My parents passed on and God called Kathy home. We bought two farms, were involved in the bus business, and sold all of the subdivision lots. The Lord is so good, seeing us through those years of happy times, times of stress, times of grief and of course the everyday work.

Where was I in my walk with the Lord during this time? I did not forget that I was a redeemed saint, yet I confess I didn't seem to grow much. God was with us all the way and sustained us through the death of our loved ones. I know part of my problem was the continual question of how to get back to the farm. I don't like to keep mentioning this, but it is true. Right or wrong I did give it a lot of thought.

II Timothy 1:12 says "For I KNOW whom I have believed and am persuaded that He is able to keep that which I have committed unto Him against that day." Praise the Lord. I want to stress the "know" in that verse. The apostle Paul reminds us in I Peter 2:11 that we are strangers, pilgrims and aliens in this world. He tells us we are a chosen people and we are on a walk and journey to our heavenly home.

While attending a funeral in Indiana one day some time during the late nineties I met a good friend, Jim Guthrie. Jim and I grew up in the same neighborhood so we knew each other well. After I left the farm in 1951, Jim got acquainted with Mary Ethel and after a while they were married. As I was talking with Jim at the funeral he said Mary would like to see me and urged us to come to their home in Bedford.

I told Margaret about the invitation for us to see Jim and Mary and we visited them. What a pleasant surprise it was to talk with them and find out that both Jim and Mary Ethel had trusted Christ as their Savior and were living for the Lord. I had not seen either of them since I left for Alaska and did not know anything about what they were doing.

What a joy it was to share how the Lord had called us to Himself. They were faithful and active in the local church. They had a good marriage with three grown children. Jim was the owner and manager of E and M Machine Tool Company in Bedford. Mary Ethel had gone to nurses training and worked as a nurse in the hospital in Bedford for a number of years.

We had such a good time, talking, praying and praising the Lord, that we returned often. We learned early on that Mary Ethel had a fast growing cancer plus a back injury from an accident. She maintained a positive witness for the Lord through this trying time in her life. The cancer was taking her strength and it was obvious she would not live long. The last time we visited she did not know us. We had prayer for Mary and the family and soon after that she was in the presence of the Lord. I occasionally see Jim and have prayer with him. I praise the Lord that God provided a good husband for Mary and a godly wife for me, though our mothers thought Mary and I should get married.

Timber Sale

On the advice of a state forester I decided to have a timber sale on the farm in the year 2000. Another forester, Brian Cruser, went through the whole forest marking the trees to be sold. He checked each tree that was marked, estimating the board feet in it and noting whether it was veneer quality. The job is easier said than done, as he had to examine over 200 hundred acres of timber land. I remember Dennis and Celesta Richardson (Marlin's sister and husband) were visiting us at the time and this was interesting to Dennis as he is from Washington, where big timber grows.

When that job was done, Brian advertised the timber sale with the number of trees and quality, including the few veneer trees. This was a sealed bid sale to be opened on a certain day. I had no idea what to expect from the sale, but Brian told me I might be surprised at the prices bid for the timber. I knew several logging companies were interested because they had come to the farm to look at the trees and the lay of the land.

This sale was a select cut, not a clear cut so I would have a good supply of trees to sell later. As we gathered in the forester's office, it was a tense time because we were anxious to see who the highest bidder was. I had the option to reject any or all of the bids if I did not like what was bid.

I was surprised both at the prices bid and how close they were to each other. It reminded me of when I submitted a proposal to the Mat-Su School District and how tense we were, waiting to see if we were in business or not. The highest bid was much more than I expected and a real blessing for us.

Churches

During this time Margaret and I often stayed all winter at the farm. While there we went to the White River Baptist Church where my parents had attended when they were living. When the pastor resigned many of the congregation left. One Sunday there was no teacher for the men's Sunday school class, as this fellow had also left. As we sat there deciding what to do, the men turned to me and said, "You take the class." The Lord said to me, "You do this because you can do it. You've sat in church all of your life and never said a word." I didn't hear an audible voice, but all the same I knew it was from the Lord. So I accepted this word from the Lord and started teaching. This was a new experience for me since I had never taught a class before. As I gained experience and confidence I began to enjoy the class.

People continued to leave, so the deacons decided to combine the men's, women's and young people's classes, keeping me as the teacher. This was a completely new challenge for me. The first Sunday I was to teach this much larger class, I waited until the very last minute to enter the classroom, thinking that I just couldn't possibly go in there and stand before all those people. I was sure to fall flat or not be able talk at all. Talk about being beyond my comfort zone! Fortunately there was a pulpit to lean on. I had studied the lesson well, so that really helped. I managed to get started and the next thing I knew it was time to dismiss for the morning church service. After this somewhat shaky start I came to look forward to the next Sunday.

White River had a problem of keeping a pastor for any length of time. A young pastor came with a fine wife and a handicapped son. I thought he was doing very well, but he didn't think so. I remember he was teaching on Wednesday night from the book of Ephesians and doing well with the lessons. One man said he wished the pastor would get out of the book of Ephesians and on to something else. I thought to myself that what the pastor was teaching was just what the man needed. After a while the situation deteriorated to the point that he had to leave. I met with the young pastor to pray with him before he preached his last sermon. The gist of the conversation was about the problem of Masons in the church.

In the meantime I had been voted in as a deacon in the church and was also on the pulpit committee. One fine man came to preach and be considered as our pastor. He gave a good message and after his sermon he opened the meeting for questions from the congregation. I asked the preacher if he would allow men who were members of the Masonic Order to hold office in the local church. The reason I asked this question was that I had done some study on the Masonic Order. I had been in contact with a couple in Salt Lake City who had been Mormons. I found out that the Mormon and Mason ceremonies and rituals are quite similar.

The poor fellow did not know how to answer the question because he was not familiar with the Masonic Order. The question set off a fire storm of loud protests defending the Masonic Lodge. Until then I was not aware of how many men in the church were Masons. One man was so angry he rose up, marched to the front of the church all the while talking in the defense of the Masons. This fellow was livid, he was so angry and upset. He was also a friend whom I had known most of my life. I thought of Psalm 41:9, "Yea, mine own familiar friend in whom I trusted, who did eat my bread, has lifted up his heel against me." I felt betrayed.

When the pulpit committee met after the service I tried to explain why I asked that question. I got nowhere with that and realized it was no use to go further with the question. One young man said, "I'm a Mason, my father is a Mason, my grandfather was a Mason and I don't see anything wrong with the Masons!"

As a result of that question I was so discouraged that I could not teach the class. I asked a friend, Kenny Dalton, if he would take my place for a while. Kenny understood and agreed to take the class. At this time we decided it was time to return to our Alaska home. We prayed about what to do when we returned to the farm next spring. The more we prayed the more certain we became that we should seek another church.

When we returned to the farm, the pastor of White River Church, and another man came to see us. We explained to the men that we felt the Lord would have us seek another church fellowship. After the meeting I called Kenny Fisher, pastor of Fairview Community Church, about coming to their fellowship. Brother Kenny told me that when Margaret and I walked into their church the first time, they sensed the presence of the Lord was with us. Those are his words, not mine. Kenny Fisher, his wife Judy, and members of Fairview Community gave us a warm welcome to their fellowship.

I look at my time and experiences at White River Baptist as a member, Sunday school teacher, deacon and a member of the pulpit committee like a milestone and turning point in my life. I sensed the presence of the Lord in a way that was much more real than before. It seemed that in the past, the Lord had to push, pull and prod to get me to do things for him. When I accepted the challenge of teaching and stepped out of my comfort zone it was a great blessing.

Another stretching experience occurred in March of 2002, while we were in Alaska. I turned eighty years old and was asked if I would tell the Spring Creek Bible Church congregation how I came to Christ. Praying that God would guide me in the right words to say that would bring praise to Him, I agreed to this request. I remember the first thing I said when I went up front was how my conversion was all of God and how He crowded me to Himself. The Lord was with me as I spoke, giving calmness of spirit and the words to say. This was a positive experience for me to be able to stand before the congregation and tell how all this came about. I have since shared my testimony in other churches. Praise His Name.

I want to say that because God chose to speak to me in such a wonderful, powerful, even frightening way at salvation does not mean that I am more special than anyone else. We are all sinners and God calls each of us in different ways. I know some who say they don't know the exact day when they were saved, but they are sure of their salvation. The very best thing a person can do is to trust Christ as a young person. Think of all the blessings of walking with the Lord throughout one's life. On the other hand think of the wasted years some of us lost forever—years of sorrow, pain, confusion and unhappiness.

My Faithful Wife

I must write about Margaret, my faithful wife. Without the Lord and Margaret I would have no story to write about. Proverbs 18:22 says "He who finds a wife finds what is good and receives favor from the Lord." This is a true statement. Margaret was always so faithful, so patient, never demanding. In fact she was the spiritual leader in our family. There were times when the children were in high school and I was driving the bus that I hardly saw them until evening. I would start the bus run before they got up so there was no time for morning devotions with the kids. Margaret prepared breakfast for me before I left with the bus, then she had time with the children before school. Margaret was a very disciplined person. Her motto was "Beds, floors and dishes done by nine o'clock" each morning.

In the early years of our marriage we had little money to live on and were practically broke. Margaret never complained about our housing, such as it was. At one time I had sawed three-sided logs for a new house. I stacked the logs near the saw mill to dry. As the logs started to dry they twisted and became bowed out of shape. They were eventually used for other things.

Another time I began to lay the forms for a new house when I stepped on a nail which went all the way through my foot. I spent a week soaking my foot in salt water to help heal the wound. That ended the project; it seemed like something always happened that kept me from building a house. Either the lumber sold or there was no time to build.

Margaret always had plenty to do—taking care of the home and garden, teaching Sunday school and ladies Bible studies, and sometimes helping at the VHS office. She had vivid memories of the Great

Depression, which caused her to be very frugal in everything she did. John Gillespie told me before we got married that I could go into debt to marry her, because she was so careful. I know she loved me more than I deserved.

In later years when we lived on the farm, Margaret called a few of the neighbor ladies together for a Bible Study. She was always the missionary wherever we went. This was a good outreach into the community for Margaret. She would walk several miles to visit some of the homes.

Margaret loved her garden whether on the farm or in Alaska. She loved to can, freeze and dry all kinds of stuff. In both homes we had a root cellar where we stored the produce. The cellar in Indiana was a concrete pre-fab that we placed in a hole where two 500 gallon fuel tanks had been. This gave us a freeze-proof place for storing canned goods and potatoes, as well as a safe place to go in case of a tornado.

Alzheimer's

The year 2000 was the last garden Margaret helped with. That spring as we were planting the seeds, Margaret fell and could not get up. I helped her to her feet and the next thing I knew she had fallen again. Setting her on her feet again, I told her that she would have to give up gardening. She accepted this new situation in her life with no complaints. I did the canning that year with her help. This ended her garden days. I did not realize at the time that it was the beginning of her battle with Alzheimer's.

It soon became evident Margaret was having some problems. Our doctor in Bedford, Dr. Childress, confirmed that she did have Alzheimer's disease. One day when I came from work she was nowhere to be found. Not knowing where to look first, I remembered that sometimes she would walk to the mail box at the end of our driveway. I started down the county road, when a pickup truck came by with Margaret in it. Two young men from Ft. Ritner were on their way home when they found her walking down the road in her stocking feet, carrying her shoes. They did not know her or where she came from. I think she was so confused that she had no idea where she was or the way home.

After this episode I didn't leave her by herself. With medication, she did seem to be somewhat better, but I knew it was time for us to be with our family in Alaska, where I could have help. The fall before I realized she had a problem, I had suggested we go to our Alaska home and she immediately said, "I won't go!" That took me by surprise as she had never talked like that before. I told her if she wanted to stay we would stay. She almost died that winter, once from pneumonia and another time she nearly choked on a piece of chicken. I grabbed her and got the piece dislodged.

After these events I knew we needed to leave the farm and return to Alaska to be near our children, so we flew up together in July of 2001. At this point the old house we had lived in for many years was gone but I realized that the trailer that replaced it would be a difficult place for Margaret to live because of her condition. She needed a home without steps, so we decided to build a house on Marlin and Sharon's property. We stayed in a friends' motorhome until our new house was finished. After getting Margaret settled in the motorhome, I flew back to the farm and packed up our belongings. Marlin was driving a school bus to Alaska, so we loaded it with our things and I rode up with him. Margaret was well taken care of by the family while I was gone.

It was a sad day when Marlin and I pulled out of the farm. Both Margaret and I had come to love our church fellowship, our neighbors and the farm. I knew Margaret would never be back with her friends and didn't know if I would either. We drove down Leesville Road and stopped for a few teary minutes with our dear friend, Pam Terrill, before we headed north.

Marlin kept up a steady pace, covering many miles each day. The first part of the trip was very hot. As we drove into Canada we couldn't seem to find a good stopping place. After finally arriving in Moose Jaw, SK, we parked behind a Wal-Mart store. We were so tired we hardly noticed where we were. The next morning I was up early and noticed on the back of the store in big letters, the name "Marlin." We got a chuckle out of that.

After returning home, we drew up house plans and started building. A few years earlier some of our friends told us that if we ever wanted to build a new house they would help. They were true to their word and went to work. The Indiana timber sale provided the funds for the house material. It was an interesting time going to Palmer and Wasilla to buy the supplies—a few hundred here, a few thousand there and a few more thousand at other stops! Many people were part of the process—Brian, Dan and Marlin were there regularly; Tim Gillespie came with his construction trailer and parked it on our site; Mike DenBleyker did a marvelous job laying out the frame. Others came by to help as well. I usually stood out of the way unless I was needed.

It was late October when we moved in and the very day we moved into the house it turned cold and wintery. We could see the hand of the Lord in all of this, getting us here, the timber sale to provide funds for the house, for friends who helped with the building and then moving into the house just as it turned cold. I am so thankful for this house and for the folks who helped with it. Even though Margaret never recognized that this was our home, she was warm and comfortable there.

There were many challenges in caring for Margaret. One Sunday I had her all dressed for church when she was stricken with diarrhea. I had to start all over again, taking off her clothes, giving her a shower, then dressing her again. This was just one episode we had. It was the daily-ness of medications, bathing and preparing food she could eat that was challenging. She took a liking for Progresso clam chowder. I had to make sure it was mashed so she would not choke.

Margaret would often think about her past, such as the time she taught Bible classes at Victory Bible Camp. This was so real to her. She explained to the class that I was her husband, but told me that they wouldn't talk to her. Then she got all worked up in her mind because the class would not respond. At this point I told her, "Why don't you dismiss the class for today." That seemed to take care of the problem. I never argued with her when she experienced these times of delusion. Another time I was having a Bible Study with a neighbor in our living room when she spoke right up on a question we had on a certain verse. Both John and I told her that we appreciated her input.

In May of 2002, Margaret fell and broke her hip. While she was recovering I had to stay close by her bed to keep her from climbing out. She didn't remember that she had surgery and a pin put in her hip. Later she had to be hospitalized for a blood clot in her leg. I noticed that her foot was swollen, so we had it checked out. While we waited in the Emergency Room, she kept wiggling and squirming so we could hardly keep her on the bed. She kept saying, "I'm all right. I want to go home". A little later she said, "If I have to stay in the hospital, I want to see the menu. I want chicken!" I couldn't help but laugh—better to laugh than cry. With medication the blood clot was taken care of in time.

As the month's passed it was obvious I needed help in taking care of Margaret. At times it was around-the-clock care. A friend from down the highway, Trish Weese, came to our rescue. At first she drove to our home, but when Margaret needed more attention, Trish suggested taking Margaret to her house. I believe it was sometime in early 2003 that we took Margaret to Tony and Trish's house, where she had her own room for several months. Tony and Trish were very generous to help us in our need. Taking care of an Alzheimer's patient is very demanding. Someone has to be with the person all the time and that was the situation with Margaret.

We have many fond memories of Margaret's sayings, many of them humorous. One time, after a bout of choking on some food she said, "I thought I kicked the bucket, but I just turned a little pale!" Another time out of the blue she told me, "You left me in the lurch after church!" Later on, perhaps feeling weary of life, she declared, "Let me die with the Philistines!" Many Alzheimer's patients become angry or violent, but Margaret never did. She became quieter, almost like another person. It seemed that Alzheimer's revealed the true person inside—a woman of faith, with a gentle and quiet spirit.

In July, 2003, we rented a motor home and drove to Ninilchik to see Marian and Nick. The motor home provided a comfortable way for Margaret to travel. Trish drove and her mother, Margaret, Sharon and I went along. I believe Margaret knew her sister; at least they were able to see each other for a short visit. We were sure that would be the last time they would see each other until they met again in glory.

The Long Lake Accident

One time in November I was up with Margaret almost all night before I could get her to sleep. After a night of very little sleep, I drove into Palmer for some supplies. While I was in Palmer I visited Johnny Gillespie, who was in the hospital at the time. It was good to visit and pray with my brother in Christ, but while I was talking with him I began to feel very tired. At the time I didn't think of it being serious, but as I drove home I felt more tired and sleepy. When I got to King Mountain Lodge I pulled in there for a break.

After resting for a few minutes and thinking I was almost home and should be able to make it without any trouble, I started up the road. That is the last thing I remember until I felt the car going over the cliff near the upper end of Long Lake. It was too late to take any action and somehow the car went over front end first. It was a loud, bumpy ride which ended on top of a pile of huge boulders. The engine stopped and I thought, "Am I dead or what?"

I decided to get out of the car, but the doors were jammed tight. Then I noticed the window in the front door of the passenger's side was down all the way. I climbed out feet first and got away from the car in case it caught on fire, as I could smell gasoline. I had my cell phone with me so decided to call someone for help. To my surprise it worked. I called Brian and told him where I was.

In the meantime I picked up a stout stick and started climbing up the very steep slope. I looked down once when I was about half way up the hill. I never looked down again when I realized that if I slipped and fell I would be back down there by the car. I was almost up to the road when Brian and Lori arrived. Brian threw down a rope to help me the rest of the way up.

By then other people had stopped to see what all the commotion was about. One fellow was in contact with the Palmer police and asked a few questions. He asked me how old I was and when I told him I was eighty years old, he looked at me again and said he thought I was in my mid-sixties. This accident ended the career of our nice Crown Victoria car. I had just gotten it ready for winter with snow tread tires.

Once again the Lord preserved my life with no injury. When I got out of the car I checked myself out to see or feel any hurts, but didn't find anything wrong. An EMT up on the highway also checked me out—nothing. After the wreck on Long Lake I was out of a vehicle in Alaska. We had left the Honda Accord in Indiana so I would have transportation there. When our friend Arnie Hrncir pulled the car up the cliff with his tow-truck, he said it had gone 280 feet down!

Final Months

As we continued with Margaret's care we realized she was slowly getting worse. She had more difficulty eating, with the danger of choking. She had times of diarrhea and at other times her bowels would not move for days. One day she finally had a bowel movement while I was talking on the phone and told the person I needed to go as Margaret had a BM. Margaret heard me say that and she said, "Now the whole world knows I had a BM!" She understood more than we realized at times.

There came a time in the fall of 2003 when Trish was tired and sick and I was very tired also with the care and lack of sleep. At that point Brian and Lori took Margaret to their home. That way I could be at my home to get some rest. I'm thankful that Brian and Lori took care of Margaret at this time of our need. It was obvious that they were very busy with homeschooling their children, Bible studies and other activities. Noting this situation, along with the fact that I did get some rest, after a few weeks I decided it was time to bring Margaret home again. It was my prayer that the Lord would allow me to take care of Margaret at home for the remainder of her life.

We celebrated our 50th wedding anniversary November 30, 2003. We knew that she could not handle a big event, so we just had our family come to our home. We received many cards for that event. Margaret asked, "Who tipped all these people off that were sending us cards?" She read most of the cards, but would forget and read them again.

Through this difficult journey with Alzheimer's, Margaret's real character and trust in the Lord really showed. I came to know and love her in a more wonderful way than before. Sometimes she would wake up in the night confused, not knowing where she was. I would talk to her, telling her, "I am Dave Lee, your husband and you are Margaret Lee, my wife, and I love you." She would add, "The joy of your life!" Many times she would say, "I just like to hear you say it."

One of Johnny and Nadine's granddaughters, Heather Gillespie, became a good helper for us that fall. She was so kind and patient with Margaret and helped us to keep track of daily medication. Our kids did what they could to help, but that fall Marlin and Sharon were out of state for a few months of sabbatical leave. Another wonderful helper who was kind and helpful was Marina Howe. Marina had taken nurses training in Russia and came to love Margaret.

Margaret sometimes experienced a great deal of pain and we had to give her morphine for it. She kept saying, "I have pain in my gizzard!" I'd ask. "Where is your gizzard?" trying to locate the source of the pain, but none of us could locate where the pain was coming from or where the "gizzard" was either. Our doctor was understanding about her need for pain medication and helped us all he could. One problem with the morphine was that it made her so dizzy she could hardly hold her head up.

Before Margaret became bedfast she would get confused about six o'clock each evening. When this happened I just sat on the couch holding her hand and talking. I did a lot of talking until she got somewhat settled down. She would say, "I want to go home", but didn't know where home was. I would try to explain to her that this was our house and we had a nice bedroom for her, but Margaret never understood this was her home. It was so sad to see a once good mind become so confused and disoriented. She almost always remembered me, but not always the children.

There came the time when she had to be in bed all the time. She never complained or got angry. Being bedfast meant there was more to be done with her care. We were careful to make her as comfortable as possible. We were fortunate in that she didn't get any bedsores. When I got Margaret dressed for bed I would read something from the Bible. It was always interesting, though not surprising, that reading The Word had such a calming effect on her. That shows the power of God's Word.

Often I would ask Margaret if she had a verse of scripture for me. Without hesitation she would quote Romans 5:8, "But God commendeth His love toward us in that while we were yet sinners Christ died for us." Every time without fail she would say Romans 5:8, then ask me if I had a verse for her. Margaret was a woman of God's Word.

Marina and others would come to help during the day and I was there all night. This helped me as we both would give her a bath and get her dressed for the day. It was a busy routine. I am so thankful that I could do this for her after all the years she had taken care of her family. Margaret slowly grew weaker and could not eat much food. She got so thin and frail that it was hard to look at her little body, but she was still a lovely person in my sight and to our family also.

Then came the time she could no longer eat, swallow or drink water. Her system just shut down. A day or two before the Lord took her home she asked me, "Am I dying?" I said, "The Lord will take you when He is ready." I knew she was dying, but didn't want to alarm her. So I asked, "Are you afraid?" She immediately said, "No, I want to see Jesus". That thrilled my heart to hear her say that. What a powerful message and reminder for the rest of us to be prepared for eternity.

It just didn't look like Margaret could live much longer, seeing she was in such a sad state. In fact I was silently praying that the Lord would take her home to be forever with the Savior she loved. Is that a sinful prayer? In my mind it wasn't since she was in such a condition, not eating or drinking anything.

On February 9, 2004 she was more restless than usual. That night I just could not get her settled in any position. This went on all night until about 4:00 am. Finally it looked like she might be resting, so I lay down and went to sleep for a bit. I was just exhausted from the all-night session. When I woke up she was all doubled over almost on her face. I straightened her out in the bed. She was still alive, but did not respond and appeared to be in a coma.

I called Sharon and she came right over to help. I was thinking we could wash and clean her up so she might be more comfortable. I just touched her arm, then she raised one arm, dropped it down and she was with the Lord. I could not feel any pulse. I know Sharon and I were just awe-struck, sensing the presence of the Lord in that room. This was an amazing experience. I think we stood there for a minute or so. I didn't cry at that time. I shed a lot more tears before the Lord took her home than at her death.

I remembered a verse as Sharon and I stood by her bedside. Romans 6:13 says, "Neither yield ye your members as instruments of unrighteousness unto sin, but yield yourselves unto God as those that are alive from the dead and your members as instruments of righteousness unto God." Margaret had yielded herself as an instrument of righteousness unto God and she was alive from the dead. What a great and awesome God we serve. Psalm 116: 15 says "Precious in the sight of the Lord is the death of His saints." Margaret was one of His chosen ones.

We called the rest of the family with the news. We all gathered around the table praying, talking and remembering Margaret, the faithful one who had ministered to all of us. Our good friend and EMT, Brian Anderson, checked Margaret's body and verified that she was indeed with the Lord. He was such a comfort and help. He called the state troopers and the funeral home for us. Margaret and I had already made arrangements with a funeral home in Wasilla.

After some discussion it was decided to have a memorial service to honor her. As Sharon said, "Mother left a legacy for us to remember." One week later we had the service and a large crowd gathered at Glacier View Bible Church. The memorial service on February 15, 2004 was full of praise to God and a wonderful time of remembering Margaret, her good deeds and her influence on those around her.

Our nephew, Loren Leman, spoke about Margaret's life, John Gillespie shared a tribute about her and Marlin brought a Bible message. Several people from the audience spoke about how Margaret's life and testimony was a blessing to them. Lori and Kristi Lucia both sang beautifully from their hearts. The memorial service was a blessing to me and a powerful witness for the Lord.

Soon after the memorial service I decided to take a walk. For over a month before Margaret passed on I had hardly done any walking. I started out to walk the Spring Creek trail that comes near our house and leads out to Victory Road. I only got about eighty feet from our front door when I fell down in the deep snow. I could hardly believe I was so weak from the months of care for Margaret. I do not regret taking care of my godly wife, but it is a demanding and tiring job to take care of a terminally ill person. I crawled to a small bush and pulled myself up with it. After that I began to recover my strength little by little.

When Margaret and I were married November 30, 1953 we promised each other we would stay together until death do us part. Now that death has taken Margaret into Glory and our fifty years together is over, I have entered a new phase of my life. The Lord has promised to never leave or forsake us. (Roman 8:38-39) I thank the Lord for the peace. He gives to His own.

In writing the story of our lives, should we only tell about the good times, the happy moments, the blessings received and not mention the trials, the testing's and the times when we sin by hurting others? No, it would not be a true story if we only told about the good things. As believers, when we sin, we can claim I John 1:9—"If we confess our sins He is faithful and just and will forgive us our sins and purify us from all unrighteousness". I have had to do this many times over the years. Through it all, God has blessed us with a wonderful family.

Fifty years together, by God's grace!—November 2003.

Family photo, Christmas, 2008: Back row–Sharon, Marlin, Brian, Lori, Dan, Sandy, Melissa, Middle row—Jenny, Rachel, Chelsea, Jesse, Ryan, Jamie (Melissa's husband); Front row—Travis, David, Jeff.

My New Journey

Shortly after Margaret's death my sister Donna's husband passed away after a bout with cancer. About a year later Donna fell and broke her leg. Since she was living alone in Indianapolis she needed help after getting home from the hospital. I was happy to fill this need and spent three months with her, doing the household chores and cooking. Recently I found out that she had been apprehensive about having my help because she remembered what I had been like many years before. We had seen each other occasionally over the years but hadn't spent a lot of time together so she didn't know how much God had changed me from the morose person I had been. God had drawn Donna to himself also, so we had some wonderful times of talking, singing and praising God together. After I left, Donna said she felt lost in her own kitchen because I had moved things around. We had some laughs about my cooking, which was not what she was used to.

In recent years I have divided my time between Indiana and Alaska, with more time on the farm. I praise God that He has given me strength to keep working. One thing I have enjoyed is planting trees on the farm, to help with erosion control and to have timber for harvesting in future years. Marlin and Sharon helped me with a tree planting in April of 2009, when we put in 1,100 hardwoods.

God blessed us with eight wonderful grandchildren: Ryan, Melissa, Travis, Rachel, Jeff, Chelsea, Jesse and Jenny. At the time of this writing, the youngest, Jenny, is preparing to enter her Senior year of high school. Rachel just graduated from Cedarville University in Ohio and Chelsea is attending the University of Alaska. Jesse went to a year of Bible school in Oregon and the others are working: Ryan in construction and commercial fishing, Melissa as an elementary teacher, Travis in commercial fishing and Jeff as a salesman for a swimming pool company in Oklahoma. Two are married: Melissa and Jamie Schroeder married June 4, 2010, and Travis and Lindsay married September 10, 2011. As of the summer of 2012, all but Jeff are living in Alaska. So much more could be said about each one, with all their interests, activities and accomplishments. Each one is special and my prayer is that they have a life-long walk with the Lord.

God has also blessed me with wonderful friends. I have enjoyed fellowship with Kenny Fisher and Tom East, two pastors with whom I can share the joys and trials of life. Frank and Mary Earl, a couple who also attended Fairview Community Church, became close friends. I often went to their home after church and spent the afternoon with them. Frank and I had much in common—sawmills, logging, mules, dozer work, etc. Most of all we talked about the Lord. It was wonderful to have a brother and sister in Christ who loved the Lord in a real way.

Frank and Mary were hospitable and caring. When I had hernia surgery they took me into their home to stay until I felt better. When I had to quit driving they picked me up on their way to church. One time I had a bad cough and Mary insisted on taking me to the doctor. I ended up in the hospital; then Frank began to have chest pains and ended up in the same room of the hospital. Over the next couple of years his health declined until he went to be with the Lord.

Jim and Pam Terrell are another couple who have been so gracious to me. She would often send over food and do my laundry. What a blessing that God gives us friends who love him and serve others. These friends have been an example of using their God-given gifts and talents. They are not the only ones who have been kind and helpful but one cannot mention each person.

Ecuador Trip

One of the great blessings of these later years was when I went on a mission trip to Ecuador in March of 2008, with Glacier View Bible Church. I was in Indiana at the time, so I joined the team in Houston and flew to Quito from there. It was a joy to travel with this group that included Sharon and granddaughter, Melissa.

In Ecuador we met a wonderful couple, Cesar and Nancy Cortez. Cesar is an engineer who plans water systems for villages that don't have clean water. Our group was there to help and encourage the villagers as they worked to install a system. From Quito, Cesar drove us to a village near the coast, San Gregorio. On the way there we stopped to enjoy some swimming in the Pacific Ocean, though I just watched.

It was fascinating to be in a foreign country, seeing the new sights and hearing a different language. Melissa had spent her first year of college in Ecuador, so she was able to help us communicate with people.

In San Gregorio we stayed in the school buildings and slept on mats underneath mosquito nets. During the morning we helped the local people dig a ditch for a water pipe. By noon it was too hot to work so we had Bible classes and games for the children in the afternoon. In the evening Cesar had a teaching time for us, then the teens on our team would play with the kids again.

The people were friendly, but very poor. They raised shrimp in large ponds as a way to earn a living. One evening some ladies fixed us a delicious meal of rice and shrimp. We enjoyed many different kinds of fresh fruit, especially bananas.

After a few days in San Gregorio we moved on to a town high in the Andes Mountains, Carabuela. It was much cooler there because of the elevation (about 11,000 feet). Again, we dug a trench for a water line. It was interesting to watch the ladies with their long dresses get down in the trench to help dig. One thing that impressed me was the very dense sod and dark, black soil. It was obviously good soil because they grew corn and other crops anywhere they could till, even up mountainsides.

When we had finished what we could there we traveled back to Quito. The final day in Ecuador, Cesar showed us some of the old buildings in Quito, and a cathedral that was gold-plated inside. We also went to an open air market where people had all kinds of hand-crafted items to sell. I bought a hat and a nice alpaca sweater. That evening we ate at a restaurant overlooking the city.

I am so thankful to God that I was allowed to go on this mission trip, especially with Sharon and Melissa. The day after the trip I turned 86.

The Journey Continues

In my late eighties I had to quit driving. Because of Restless Leg Syndrome I often couldn't sleep at night, so it became hazardous to drive. One time in Alaska I fell asleep while driving to Palmer and crashed into Granite Creek. Fortunately no one was in the on-coming lane, but a couple noticed the splash and stopped to help. The truck ended on its side but I was able to climb out the passenger door. I was bruised and sore, and the truck was totaled. After another incident in Indiana, where I hit a mailbox, it seemed like time to give up the keys. Living without my own mode of transportation has been difficult at times. It is hard to always be dependent on others, but that is part of the journey.

One other major event was when I had heart surgery December 27, 2010. For about a year I had been losing strength, feeling breathless when walking and had a feeling of pressure in my chest. Finally a heart specialist did some tests and discovered that there were three major blockages. The doctor immediately sent me to Indianapolis by ambulance, where I had triple-bypass surgery the next day. I was impressed with the wonderful care I received at St. Vincent Heart Hospital, and how many believers worked there.

It was a long road to recovery for an 88 year-old. After ten days in the hospital I was transferred to a nursing facility in Bedford for rehabilitation. This also was a caring place and I made many new friends during my stay at Stonebridge Health Campus. It was a difficult time in life. There was the pain from surgery, plus I had a terrible cough and felt low emotionally. However, after about two months there I was ready to go home. Marlin and Sharon flew to Indiana to be with me for a couple of weeks while I transitioned to being at home.

In thinking of my life as a journey, I was reminded of some scriptures. Philippians 3:12-15 states, "Not that I have already obtained all this or have already been made perfect but I press on to take hold of that which Christ Jesus took hold of me. Brothers, I do not consider myself yet to have taken hold of it. But one thing I do: Forgetting what is behind and straining toward what is ahead, I press on toward the goal to win the prize for which God has called me heavenward in Christ Jesus." I've now passed the milestone of 90 years. My strength is waning but I am still living at home and move around without aid, though slowing down. Only God knows when my earthly journey will end, but Praise His Name, I know that when it does, I'll go to be with Him!

Dear Reader,

I do not know where you are in the journey of life, but I'd like to urge you to trust in the Lord Jesus Christ as I did. I can attest that it is worth it! Here are a few verses that tell what our condition is, what God has done for us and what our response should be:

- Romans 3:23 All have sinned and fall short of the glory of God.
- John 3:16 For God so loved the world that He gave His one and only Son, that whoever believes in him shall not perish but have eternal life.
- Romans 5:8 But God demonstrates His own love for us in this: while we were still sinners, Christ died for us.
- Acts 16:31 Believe in the Lord Jesus Christ and you will be saved.
- Romans 10:9 If you confess with your mouth, "Jesus is Lord", and believe in your heart that God raised him from the dead, you will be saved.

I pray that God will use these words to speak to you, and that you will find hope, peace and joy in Him.

A fellow traveler,

David Lee

Made in the USA
San Bernardino, CA
15 February 2014